WORLD WAR I
FACT BOOK

To Terry, Peter, and Tom

WORLD WAR I FACT BOOK

THE GREAT WAR IN GRAPHS AND NUMBERS

WILLIAM VAN DER KLOOT

AMBERLEY

First published 2010

Amberley Publishing Plc
Cirencester Road, Chalford,
Stroud, Gloucestershire, GL6 8PE

www.amberley-books.com

Copyright © William Van der Kloot, 2010

The right of William Van der Kloot to be
identified as the Author of this work has been
asserted in accordance with the Copyrights,
Designs and Patents Act 1988.

ISBN   978 1 84868 447 8

British Library Cataloguing in Publication Data.

A catalogue record for this book is available
from the British Library.

Typeset in Anselm Serif.
Typesetting and Origination by FonthillMedia.
Printed in Great Britain.

CONTENTS

ACKNOWLEDGEMENTS

I thank Judy Samarel and T.M.C. Van der Kloot for help with the manuscript. I am grateful for the assistance of the staffs of the London Library, British Library, Archives of the Imperial War Museum, Library of the Museum of the British Army, New York Public Library, Melville Library at Stony Brook University, Bodleian Library at Oxford, and the Cambridge University Library. The graphing software is CoPlot, from CoHort Software, *www.cohort.com*.

PREFACE

History is numbers as well as words and images, and the numbers should be the starting point for those trying to understand the history. The Great War produced large volumes stuffed with long columns of numbers, covering almost anything you can think of, from how many prisoners were taken in a given battle to the number of troops in each age group who contracted a venereal disease. Some of these numbers resurface in narrative histories of the war, which are dotted with data on casualties, numbers of shells fired and the like. However, it is not easy to locate the numbers in the history books, and the large volumes with columns of numbers are available only in a few major libraries.

This book makes some of the most important and revealing numbers accessible, not as long columns, but mostly as graphs, which make it easier to compare the figures for the two sides and the changes over time. The book resembles an extended PowerPoint presentation of the war, in which the graphs and numbers would flash on the screen, while the text provides the narration.

World War I was one of the most dramatic conflicts in human history. In World War II the eventual outcome was predictable after Stalingrad, El Alamein, and Midway; the last years were watching the hand being played to completion. In the First War the Central Powers seemed on the verge of victory on both land and sea in June 1918. Four months later they were desperately suing for peace.

William Van der Kloot, 2009

THE POPULATION EXPLODES

In the 18th century human energy use began to skyrocket. In Europe and the Americas people investigated farming scientifically and communicated and discussed their results. Soil preparation, tillage, drainage, and fertilizer use were studied and markedly improved. Seeds and livestock were selected for productivity and other desirable traits—the Stud Book was first published in 1791.

Consequently food production soared; it was a Second Agricultural Revolution. People who ate more worked harder. (Starving people do little work, not because they are lazy but because they cannot.) Better fed people lived longer, grew taller, and had larger families.

After centuries of slow increase, world population began to expand exponentially; this accelerated growth continues to this day[1].

The populations of the European countries expanded rapidly[2], even though many people emigrated to the New World and to African and Asian colonies to escape the crush. In several decades 10% of the British emigrated.

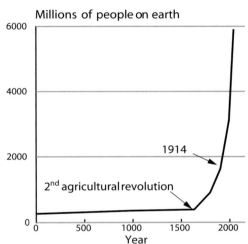

Millions of people on earth

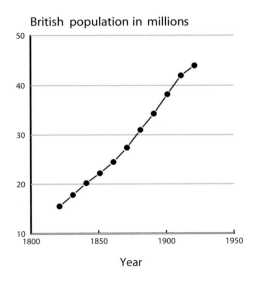

British population in millions

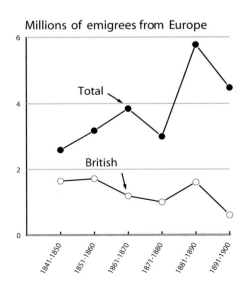

Millions of emigrees from Europe

THE INDUSTRIAL REVOLUTION

The hardworking people added to their energy supply by burning wood and coal to produce steam to operate machinery[2]. Britain was first off the mark, and built a great empire. She also led in the production of steel, but toward the end of the 19th century she was surpassed by the German Empire[2] (formed in 1871).

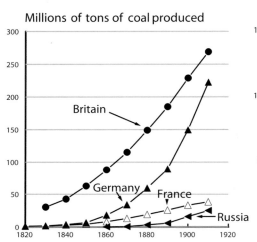

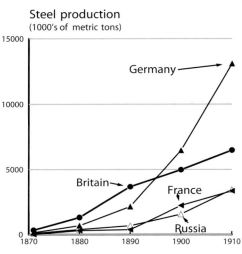

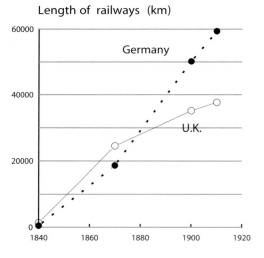

Steel was used for railways[2] and ships, both propelled by steam; they facilitated commerce. Newspaper sales boomed when prices fell thanks to steam presses and distribution by railway: in Britain circulation increased more than **400-fold** between 1821 and 1920[4].

Readers learned about politics and international affairs, and demanded more of a say. A smaller percentage of people farmed and more worked in industry in growing cities. By 1911 one third of French workers were in industry and one third of these were women[5].

GROWTH OF WEALTH

European countries became wealthier. After a lag, despite the increase in population, so did individuals[6]. The British were substantially richer than the French or Germans, but incomes rapidly increased in all three countries.

During the last half of the century real wages (which take into account changes in prices) rose substantially and continuously[2].

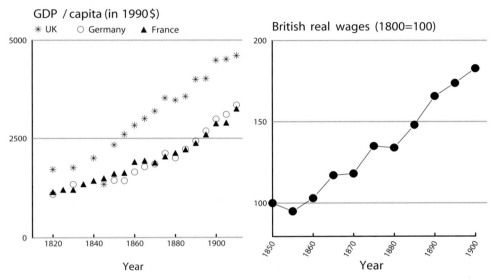

Wealth improved education. Much data on literacy depends on responses to census takers—self evaluations—but the declining percent of those unable to sign their names on English marriage registers shows unambiguous improvement[83].

Governments devoted more resources to education and science. The British were striving to catch up with the Germans in these fields[2].

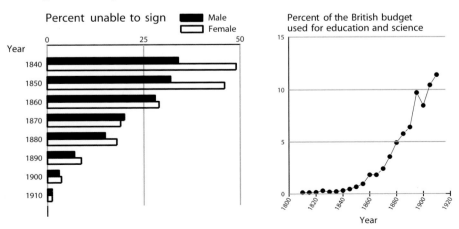

GROWTH OF EMPIRES

The major powers employed some of their newfound energy and wealth to acquire colonies and built great empires. The British used their naval strength to take over 25% of the earth's land[56]. The Russians expanded their land borders: they occupied 14% of the planet's soil. Likewise, the US continued to expand on land until the turn of the century.

Many of the empires were ambitious to grow further. The Russians, for example, had their eyes on the Dardanelles and Constantinople.

Areas of empires (sq miles)

51,000 sq km= average area added per year to the Russian Empire in the 19th century

19ᵀᴴ CENTURY WARS

In the 17th century there were only seven years of peace in Europe. After the fall of Napoleon, in the remainder of the 19th century there were many years of peace. In the wars casualties were light, only a small fraction of the population. Bloodshed was accepted as an inevitable and not unreasonable mechanism for resolving disputes between countries[7]. The American Civil War was the exception; 8.8% of the white males in the Confederacy were casualties.

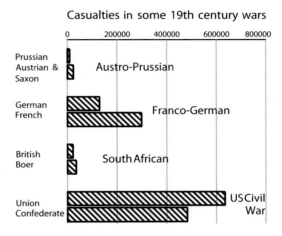

Casualties in some 19th century wars

The European countries invested part of their burgeoning wealth in weapons and in training men by compulsory military service, arguing that this was as necessary for protecting peace as it was for waging war[8]. The years of mandatory service varied, as did the years in the active reserve. Following the active reserve were various categories of older men still liable to be called up[9].

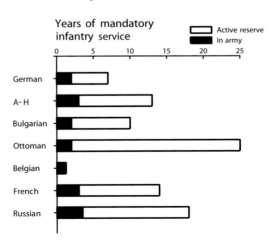

PREPARING FOR WAR

The British relied on a professional army and maintained the world's largest navy. Their military spending soared during their wars, but after 1850 it also grew in peacetime and remained at high levels after the Boer War[2]. The British army cost more than the navy for most of the 19th century, but the naval race with Germany changed that. British expenditures per person rose 2.2 fold from 1865 to 1912[81].

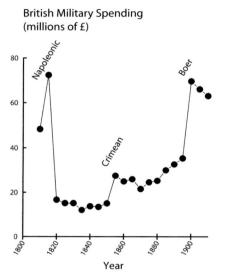

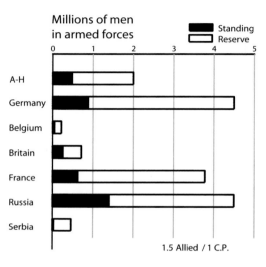

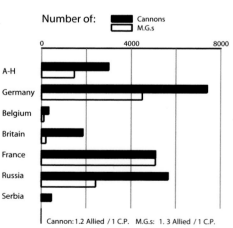

Alliances were formed to maintain a balance of power, and were considered a prerequisite for peace. France and Russia were allied, and the British had secret, non-binding agreements with the French. Austria-Hungary and Germany were allied, and Italy was pledged to join them if they were attacked. In 1914 the Italians were freed from their obligation because the Austro-Hungarians and then the Germans declared war. The Italians were promised magnificent spoils and in 1915 joined the Allies. In 1913 the war expenditures of the future Allies were more than twice those of the Central Powers (C.P.)[9]. When Serbia and Belgium found themselves on the Allied side at the outbreak, the Allies mobilized 1.5 men for every opponent.

THE OPPOSING FORCES

The odds were closer in important weapons like cannons and machine guns[9]—but still with an edge to the future Allies. The Allies started with more aeroplanes, while the Central Powers had more airships[9].

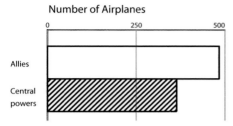

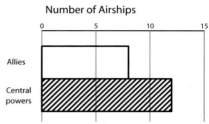

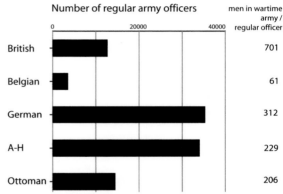

Regular army officers were a precious resource[9,10,11,12].

Also shown on the graph are how many men were in the armies at full strength for each officer they had at the outset.

	men in wartime army / regular officer
British	701
Belgian	61
German	312
A-H	229
Ottoman	206

The Allies had overwhelming superiority at sea, with many more warships and almost twice as many men in their navies[9].

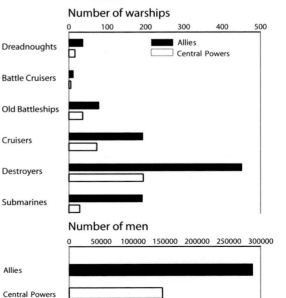

15

MEN AND WEAPONS

The physical standards for military training were high in Austria-Hungary and low in Russia[13]. In the Russian Army most of the non-commissioned officers (NCOs) were promoted from the ranks and served only during their period of training[13]. In Germany young men were recruited, schooled, and then served for twelve years as NCOs. After army service they were guaranteed state employment, many as policemen or postmen; they gave civil life a military cast. The Germans called up only about half those eligible for training. Many of their untrained men enlisted at the outbreak of war.

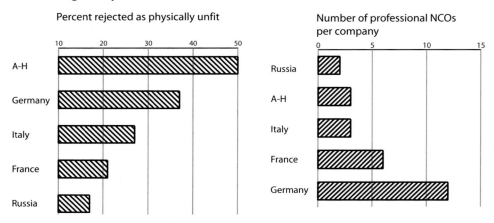

THE TERRORISTS

A terrorist threw a bomb at the heir to the Austrian and Hungarian thrones on the morning of his visit to Sarajevo, the capital of Bosnia-Herzegovina. He missed their open car and was arrested before he could take his cyanide pill. In the afternoon the Archduke's car took a wrong turn, unexpectedly stopping in front of another assassin, 19-year-old Gavril Princip. He shot husband and wife. When arrested, one of the young plotters revealed that the bombs and pistols had come from the Serbian government, who had also smuggled some of the terrorists into Bosnia-Herzegovina (map page 38). The Austro-Hungarians proposed to punish the Serbians. Their ally, the German Kaiser, gave them a 'blank cheque' to avenge his friends. The Austro-Hungarians pledged that if it came to war they would not take any Serbian territory, because the Hungarians did not want more troublesome Slavs added to the Empire.

The Austro-Hungarians presented a harsh ultimatum to Serbia. One clause demanded that they admit Austro-Hungarian investigators to ferret out government officials privy to the plot. The Serbians rejected that clause, but agreed to all else. Without further discussion the Austro-Hungarians declared war. The Russians began to mobilize; the French held firm to their alliance with Russia.

ROLLING THE IRON DICE

The Germans could not permit the Russians to get a head start. The Russians refused to stop mobilizing so the Germans declared war, because under their Constitution they had to be at war before they could mobilize. The British Foreign Secretary was saved the embarrassment of revealing his secret undertakings with the French when Germany invaded Belgium, which had refused permission for them to pass through. Britain was pledged by a treaty of 1830 to defend Belgian neutrality.

JUNE
28:     Archduke Franz Ferdinand and his wife murdered by a Serbian terrorist.

JULY
23 :   Austro-Hungarian ultimatum delivered to Serbia.
24 :   British Fleet ordered to remain mobilized at end of summer exercises.
25 :   Serbia mobilizes. Austro-Hungary partially mobilizes.
26 :   War preparation announced for European Russia.
28 :   Austro-Hungary declares war on Serbia.
29 :   Warning telegram to army and fleet in Britain. Russian partial mobilization.
30 :   Russian full mobilization.
31 :   Austro-Hungary mobilizes.

AUGUST
1 :   At 16.45 France mobilizes. At 17.00 Germany mobilizes. Germany declares war on Russia.
3 :   Germany declares war on France and invades Belgium.
4 :   Great Britain declares war on Germany.

The network of alliances set up by the statesmen to preserve peace had ensured war.

51 kg = minimum weight for a man to enlist in the British Army

MOBILIZATION

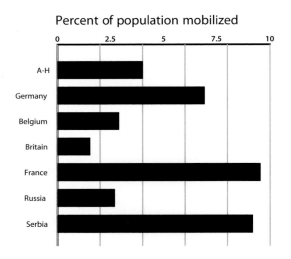

Percent of population mobilized

When the nations mobilized the French called up the highest proportion of their population, the British the lowest[9].

CANNON

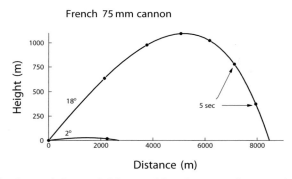

French 75 mm cannon

All of the armies had rapid-firing field guns like the French 75 and British 18-pdr[14,15], which could fire 15 shells in a minute. They were designed to fire shrapnel shells, which are canisters containing lead balls. The canister explodes in the air at a preset time after the shell is fired, spraying the balls over the ground. Shrapnel is devastating against men in the open. However, if the targets are in a trench the balls come at such a low angle that they hit the parapet. The shell weighed 5.5 kg. The range of the gun was lengthened by elevating the barrel. The 75 had a maximum elevation of 18° because it was restricted by its solid trail, which made it easy to move about. At maximum range the shell took almost 35 seconds to reach its target, while the sound of the discharge arrived in 1.6 seconds. Experienced men could tell from the sound of firing if the shell was heading their way and had time to take shelter.

HOWITZERS AND HIGH POWER GUNS

Howitzers fire at a high angle and drop shells down on the target. Usually they fired high explosive shells which detonated when they hit the ground, destroying with their blast and by the jagged shards of iron flung from their casings. They were ideal for smashing trenches. A 6-inch howitzer shell travelled for a minute or more; the sound of the firing reached the target in about 1.5 seconds. Careful tests showed that a target like a trench could be hit with fewer shots fired by a howitzer than with a field gun[64].

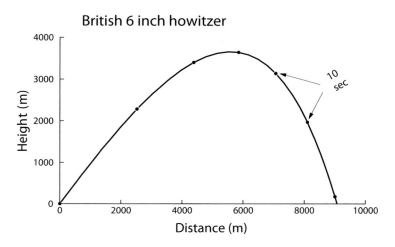

British 6 inch howitzer

As the war went on, both sides developed guns with high muzzle velocities, like the French 155-mm, which fired a 43.1-kg shell. They also designed shells that minimized air resistance at supersonic speeds. These guns were so well engineered that the basic designs were used in World War II.

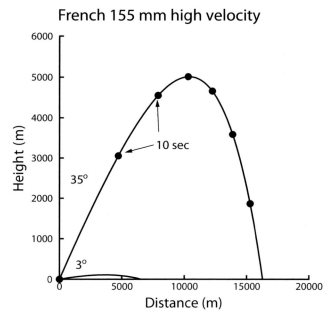

French 155 mm high velocity

LONG RANGE GUNS AND MORTARS

The most spectacular pieces were the elongated German naval guns mounted on railway carriages that bombarded Paris in 1918[16]. They were raised to a fixed elevation of 50° and the range was determined by the charge of explosive used to fire the shell; the pressure inside of the firing chamber was measured with each shot. The shells shot up into the stratosphere, where the air resistance is low. The shells weighed 120 kg. Spies reported where the shells fell, because Paris was too well defended to permit aeroplane spotting in daylight.

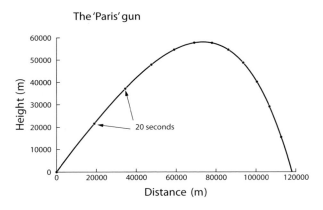

The 'Paris' gun

Mortars use a relatively small charge to fire a shell a short distance. Some mortars fired shells the size of oil barrels, containing 95 kg of high explosive. Such slow moving shells were easily seen, giving the quarry a few seconds to scramble to safety, so often they would be simultaneously targeted with shrapnel. Design was revolutionized in 1916 by the British Stokes mortar: its shell is fired when it is simply dropped into the tube. It was light and mobile enough to be brought forward by attackers.

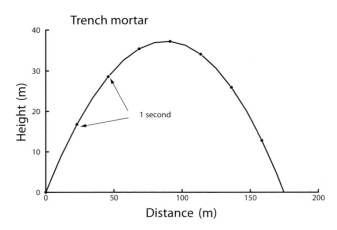

Trench mortar

MACHINE GUNS AND MOBILE HEAVY GUNS

Machine guns fired rapidly, up to 600 bullets per minute, but required trained gun teams for maximum effectiveness. In the diagram the gun is mounted 2 m above the ground. The 2 m height is shadowed to show the region in which a bullet might strike a standing man. At short range everyone is at risk, but at longer ranges the danger area is smaller. Therefore the gunners needed good range estimates.

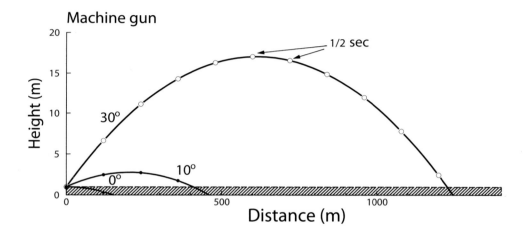

The opening weeks of the war revealed that the Central Powers had a pivotal advantage: they had far more and far better mobile heavy guns to use against fortresses and in the field[15,52,53]. They were unexpected, terrifying, and devastating.

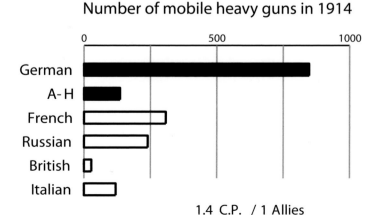

Number of mobile heavy guns in 1914

1.4 C.P. / 1 Allies

CAUSES OF WOUNDS

The British data on wounds by different weapons show that artillery did the most damage[17]. Wounds from rifles and machine guns could not be distinguished. Few were wounded by the bayonet, though in 1916 the British issued an illustrated manual of technique which was not to be taken into the trenches for fear that these secrets would be revealed to the enemy[19]. In the early part of the war the British infantry advanced in line, so they would reach the enemy trench simultaneously for their bayonet attack.

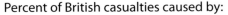

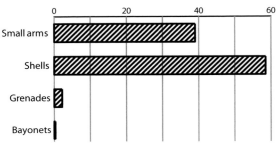

The German figures are quite similar to the British, despite the Germans fighting rather different wars in East and West. Characteristically, the German categories are more precise[18]. Again artillery did most damage.

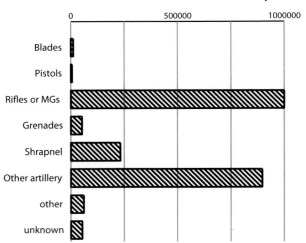

Barbed wire was widely used after 1867 when a machine to fabricate it was invented in Illinois. It transformed stock farming. Neither side expected it to become one of the major weapons of the Great War.

THE WEST IN 1914

The French, commanded by Joseph Joffre, mobilized rapidly and launched an all-out attack to drive the Germans out of the 'lost' provinces of Alsace and Lorraine, taken by the Germans in 1871. They suffered enormous casualties: 18% of their killed and missing were lost in the first two months of the war [5,9]. They lost 2.7 men for every German killed or missing on their front.

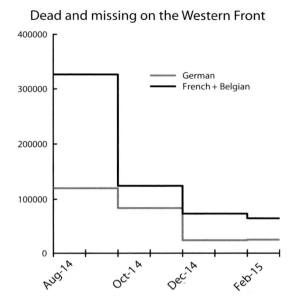

Dead and missing on the Western Front

The Germans, battling on two fronts, followed the plan devised years before by Schlieffen: they concentrated their forces in the west, planning to defeat the French before dealing with the Russians. Neutral Belgium refused to let the Germans pass through, so they invaded, smashing the Belgian frontier forts with heavy howitzers. From Brussels, the German right wing swung south to take the French army and their strongest frontier forts from the rear. The British moved their small expeditionary force, the BEF, commanded by Sir John French, to the French left flank. The German plan was for their left wing, in Alsace and Lorraine, to withdraw if pushed hard to lure the French deeper into the trap. Instead the German commander, Helmuth von Moltke, permitted his left wing to fight for ground and even to counter-attack[73].

In the original plan, 13% of the German troops were to be in the left wing; Moltke had 29% there[18]. He also took men away from his right wing in the West to reinforce the Eastern Front, where they arrived after the crucial battle was fought (page 31). As the campaign progressed, the number of men in the right wing decreased far more than the number in the left wing, which was sustained almost to the level at the outset. We will never know whether Moltke's changes altered the result.

163 = number of trains the French used to move troops back from east to west for the Marne[52]

THE GERMAN ARMIES IN THE WEST

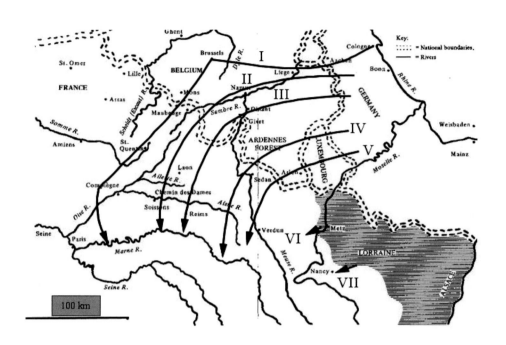

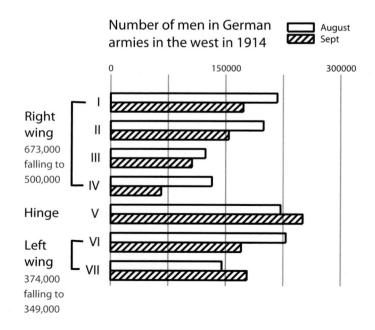

Number of men in German armies in the west in 1914

Key:
- ⬜ August
- ▨ Sept

Right wing
673,000 falling to 500,000
- I
- II
- III
- IV

Hinge
- V

Left wing
374,000 falling to 349,000
- VI
- VII

24

THE SCHLEIFFEN PLAN

Joffre stopped his futile attacks in the east and shifted troops westward by railway, a bold and hazardous manoeuvre during a great battle. The German right wing swept down from Belgium, driving the British and the French before them, defeating the BEF at Mons and Neuve Chapelle and the French at Guise. The German right wing marched and fought over an extensive distance, their I Army had the furthest to go. Its right flank swung north of the fortifications of Paris and turned southeast. The Germans cut two of the main railway trunk lines from Paris to the eastern frontier and were within striking distance of the line in the Seine valley. However, as they marched forward, a 30 km gap opened between their I and II Armies[73].

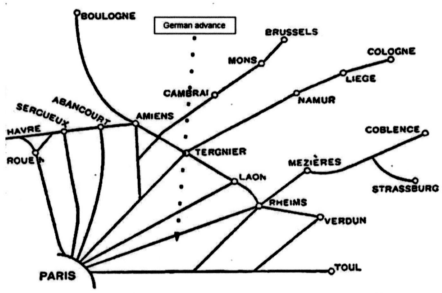

MAIN LINES - PARIS to North and to Battle Front

Distances for German I Army at the Marne (km)

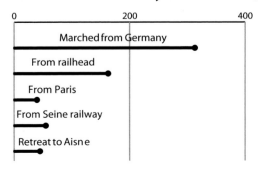

FIRST BATTLE OF THE MARNE

Sir John French proposed to withdraw the BEF to the channel coast. He was persuaded to stand and to join the French in a do-or-die counter-attack along the River Marne. The French also struck the German right flank with the garrison from Paris, a handful of them—famously—brought to the battle by taxi[73]. Moltke remained far in the rear because he was also responsible for the Eastern Front. His armies reported to him by short, coded wireless messages. The Allies advanced slowly into the gap between the German armies. Moltke sent an intelligence officer to evaluate the situation. This officer ordered the I & II armies to retreat, overruling the objections of the I Army commander. Moltke, his nerves shattered, confirmed his aide's order and withdrew his entire right wing to defensive positions in northern France along the River Aisne. Therefore, during most of the crucial battle of the Marne the Germans were withdrawing and the Allies attacking—but advancing too cautiously to seriously disrupt the German retreat. The Germans engineers prepared a defensive line along the heights of the river Aisne (map page 66).

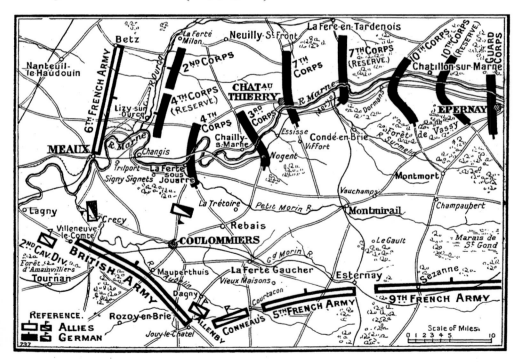

Casualty figures for the Marne battle itself are speculative; the best information available is the total figures for the first months of the war in the west[48]. As usual the ratio of the casualties on the two sides is shown on the graph.

CASUALTIES IN THE WEST

Looking at the percentages killed in the seven German armies in the first two months of the war shows how the intensity of the battle in the West shifted from the left wing (VI and VII armies) to the right (I, II, and III armies)[18]. The V army was the hinge. The VIII army was in the east.

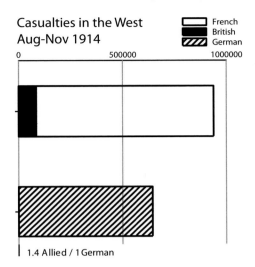

Casualties in the West Aug-Nov 1914

French
British
German

1.4 Allied / 1 German

Percent of German armies killed in:

August   September

Moltke was replaced by Erich von Falkenhayn, though for weeks both this change and the withdrawal were concealed from the public. The Germans beat back strong attacks on their defensive position along the Aisne and then shifted the battle to Flanders, trying to take the transportation hub of Ypres and to occupy the coast of the English Channel. The cream of the German Army and tens of thousands of slightly trained volunteers were thrown against the Allied trenches in the battle known as First Ypres. They could not prevail. The BEF also lost heavily[9] (page 31).

FIRST YPRES

The German Western front in the Winter of 1914.

(The place names on this map are in German spelling.)

Finally Falkenhayn ordered his armies to go on the defensive in the West and to dig in on favourable ground. Soon the trenches ran from the Channel to the Swiss frontier[75]. By the end of the year, the French were futilely striking at the German line in Champagne, trying to drive the invaders out of France. Total Allied casualties (killed, wounded, prisoners and missing) were **1.5** times greater than German[9,10].

Casualties on Western Front through January 1915

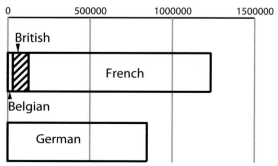

1.5 Allied / 1 German

SERBIA IN 1914

In the east the Austro-Hungarians invaded Serbia (map on page 38) but were balked by stout resistance—demonstrating what could be expected from the polyglot, multilingual Austro-Hungarian army on the offensive[9].

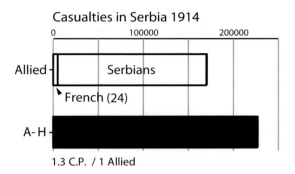

Casualties in Serbia 1914

THE EASTERN FRONT IN 1914

The Russians mobilized rapidly, which forced the Austro-Hungarians to shift most of their troops from Serbia to the frontier of their province of Galicia (now the southern part of Poland). From there the Austro-Hungarians advanced into the Tsar's Grand Duchy of Poland (now central Poland), but were soon driven back and Galicia was invaded in turn. Both sides suffered enormous losses in the battle of Lemberg[9].

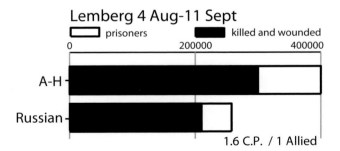

Lemberg 4 Aug-11 Sept

The Russians also launched two uncoordinated armies into German East Prussia (now northern Poland). One came north from Warsaw; the other advanced west from Vilnius (now in Lithuania). Each army advanced along a railway line, which, since the German and Russian railways had different gauges, ended at the frontiers. The Germans had a single army of **210,000 men** in the East. Its commander panicked, so he was replaced by Paul von Hindenburg, called out of retirement, with Erich Ludendorff as his chief-of-staff.

POLAND, PRUSSIA, AND GALICIA

The Eastern front in 1914[73].

TANNENBERG

The Germans used their railway network to concentrate against the Russian Warsaw army. This was an obvious move. The brilliance of the new commanders was revealed when they allowed the Russians to push a thin screen of older reservists back deep into East Prussia, meanwhile massing troops on each flank. They encircled and destroyed the invaders at Tannenberg[9,13]. Then they turned and drove the Vilnius army out of East Prussia with heavy losses.

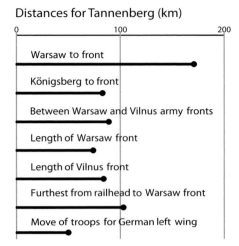

Distances for Tannenberg (km)

The comparison between casualties in the East and West—Tannenberg and First Ypres (page 27)—is revealing[9].

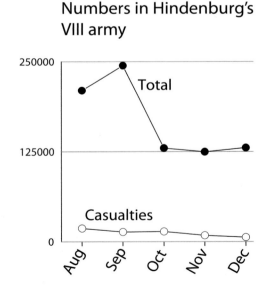

Casualties at First Ypres

British
French
Belgian
German

1.3 C.P. / 1 Allied

Casualties at Tannenberg

Russian

German

11 Allied / 1 C.P.

Numbers in Hindenburg's VIII army

Total

Casualties

1,500 = number of letters Hindenburg wrote to his wife Gertrude during the war

CASUALTIES IN THE EAST

The Russian, Serbian, and Austro-Hungarian armies sustained a mind-boggling number of casualties on the Eastern Front in 1914[9].

Casualties on Eastern Front in 1914

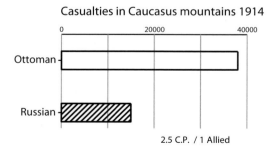

1.3 Allied / 1 C.P.

THE OTTOMANS AND THE JAPANESE

The Ottoman Empire joined the Central Powers. This did not disturb either the British, who regarded them as a pushover holding valuable property, or the Russians, who wanted Constantinople. The British promptly occupied the city of Basra and the nearby oil fields in what now is southern Iraq. Oil was vital as fuel for the new warships in the British fleet. The Ottomans battled the Russians along the frontier in the Caucasus mountains, and were defeated badly [9,12]. The Ottoman army there was commanded by the minister of war, Enver Pasha, one of the three "young Turks" who controlled the government.

Casualties in Caucasus mountains 1914

2.5 C.P. / 1 Allied

The Japanese entered the war on the Allied side, which enabled the Russians to withdraw most of their troops from their eastern frontier. The Japanese and Australian fleets raced to seize the German islands in the Pacific. The Japanese also besieged Tsingtao (now Qingdao), a German treaty port on the coast of China. The outnumbered Germans surrendered, giving the Japanese a substantial foothold in China[9]. The Japanese politely declined requests to send troops to the Western Front, but did contribute some anti-submarine vessels to the Allied efforts in the Mediterranean.

CHINA

Total Allied casualties for 1914 were **1.3 times** those of the Central Powers; total losses by both sides in the East were **1.6 times** those in the West[10].

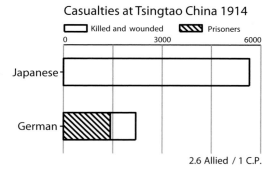

Casualties at Tsingtao China 1914

☐ Killed and wounded ▨ Prisoners

2.6 Allied / 1 C.P.

AFRICA

The Germans had four colonies in Africa, acquired in 1884-85[82]. Togoland (now Togo and parts of Ghana and Benin) was invaded by British and French from their adjoining colonies[54]. The Germans surrendered at the end of August. Cameroon (now Cameroon and part of Nigeria) was invaded by the British and French who landed near the principal harbour and captured the town and radio station. The Germans retreated into the interior where they continued to resist until the following spring. In South-West Africa (now Nambia) the Germans abandoned the ports and retreated into the interior. The prime minister of South Africa, General Louis Botha, once a Boer general, promised to maintain British interests so they could send their 6,000 man garrison to France. Some Boers rebelled, but they were defeated by Botha and Boers loyal to Britain, who also occupied the coast of South-West Africa.

The Germans had a force of about **10,000** in German East Africa (now mainland Tanzania, Rwanda, and Burundi), commanded by Colonel Paul von Lettow-Vorbeck. The British had few troops in Uganda and British East Africa, so an Indian Army force landed on the coast. They were defeated and withdrew, abandoning a substantial store of arms and munitions[9].

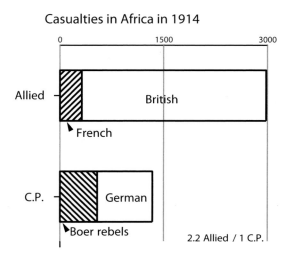

Casualties in Africa in 1914

2.2 Allied / 1 C.P.

1915 IN THE WEST

The Western Front 1/1/1915

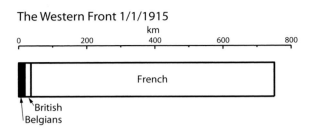

At the beginning of 1915 most of the Allied trench line was held by the French[9]. The Germans worked to improve their defences, digging deep and constructing concrete pillboxes and observation posts. The Allies were less concerned about their fortifications, which they regarded as jumping off lines for re-conquering lost ground.

WESTERN BATTLEFIELDS

Toward the end of winter Joffre tried again to break through the German lines in Champagne and Artois, north of Arras, to gain the Notre Dame de Lorette ridge[73]. Next Falkenhayn attacked near Ypres again, completely surprising the Allies and breaking their line by using a cloud of poisonous chlorine gas released from cylinders. The breakthrough was not exploited. The German infantry advanced to their pre-determined stop line and dug in; the attack was a diversion for the main German thrust in the East[38]. The Allies counter-attacked and the battle degenerated into another bloody standoff[9].

On the map to the left, the arrowhead from Ypres indicates the direction of the British attack in 1917; the arrowhead from Lille shows the direction of the German attack over the river Lys in 1918.

2nd YPRES AND ARTOIS

8=

number of Germans who worked on gas warfare who had won or were to win the Nobel Prize [38]

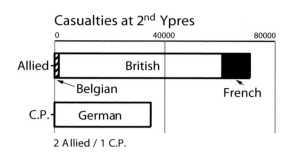

Casualties at 2nd Ypres

2 Allied / 1 C.P.

In the next joint Allied attack Sir John French failed to take the Aubers Ridge and the French were blocked again in Artois, charging vainly up the heights north of Arras[9]. Barbed wire, machine guns, and trenches dominated the battlefield.

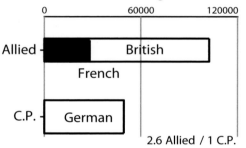

Casualties at Aubers Ridge and 2nd Artois

2.6 Allied / 1 C.P.

LOOS

Sir John blamed his defeat on a shortage of artillery ammunition. He was replaced by a subordinate, Sir Douglas Haig. In the autumn another joint Allied attack failed, the British suffering heavily at Loos, where they disastrously bloodied some of the troops raised and trained since the outbreak of the war[9].

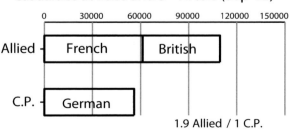

Casualties at Loos and 3rd Artois (Sep-15)

1.9 Allied / 1 C.P.

CASUALTIES IN THE WEST 1915

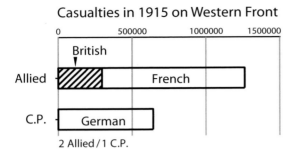

Casualties in 1915 on Western Front

2 Allied / 1 C.P.

During 1915 in the West the Germans, largely on the defensive, suffered far less than the Allies[9].

12,000= number of bullets fired by one German machine gun at Loos[27]

THE EAST IN 1915

At the beginning of the year the Russians were edging the Austro-Hungarians back through the passes of the Carpathian Mountains, threatening to break through to the Hungarian plain. To relieve the pressure the Germans attacked in the north, despite the winter snows and ice. They won great tactical victories—at Mansuria for example[9]—but the Russians were not deterred by their losses.

120,000= number of Austro-Hungarians surrendered when the Russians captured the fortress of Przemysl[53]

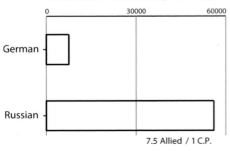

Casualties at Mansuria (Feb 1915)

7.5 Allied / 1 C.P.

To keep his faltering allies in the war, Falkenhayn undertook a joint attack with the Austro-Hungarians. They concentrated their artillery and formed a combined army commanded by a German, August Mackensen, which broke though the weak trench line defending the Russian right flank, extending between the towns of Gorlice and Tarnow (map on page 30). Then they advanced, averaging 16 km per day, pushing the Russians before them.

GORLICE-TARNOW

They were aided by attacks in the north by Hindenburg's army. Warsaw fell and the Russians were pushed out of most of Poland. The fronts were long and the Central Powers pushed them far to the east[9].

Distances for Poland 1915 (km)

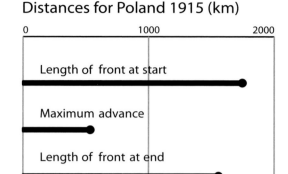

1,600 = number of Russian guns lost when the Germans took the fortress of Novogeorgievsk [53]

As the Russians retreated they devastated the land, just as their ancestors had done when the French invaded in 1812. They drove the civilians before them, every ethnic group residing in Poland[9]. The Jews were coerced to leave with the others and along the road they were assaulted, raped, and murdered in vicious pogroms[53].

Number and ethnicity of refugees on Eastern Front

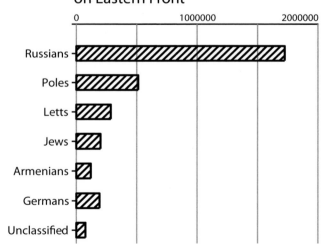

25,450 kg = weight of an Austro-Hungarian Skoda MI9II howitzer[54]

THE FALL OF SERBIA

Later in the year the Germans, Austro-Hungarians, and Bulgarians, who had entered the war, attacked the Serbs with a combined army commanded by Mackensen. The French and British were unable to help. Serbia[73] was overwhelmed and the surviving defenders were evacuated by sea[9].

CASUALTIES IN THE EAST IN 1915

Casualties in Serbia 1915

The Central Powers were the clear victors in the East in 1915. Moreover, they had shortened their front substantially by destroying Serbia[9].

Casualties on Eastern Front in 1915

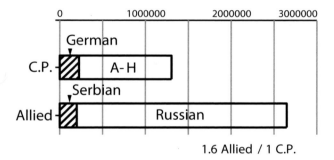

1.6 Allied / 1 C.P.

THE MIDDLE EAST IN 1915

During the depth of the winter the Ottomans were defeated for a second time by the Russians in the Caucasus Mountains[12]. The weather in which they fought was so terrible that casualties due to frostbite were recorded separately.

Caucasus Mountains, early 1915

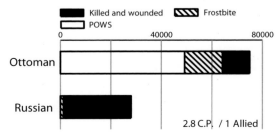

2.8 C.P. / 1 Allied

THE DARDANELLES

In February 1915 an Allied fleet of out-of-date battleships was unable to force its way through the Dardanelles. In April British and French troops were landed on the Gallipoli Peninsula to take the defending forts from the rear. The Ottoman defenders, aided by a few German specialists and commanded by a German general, held the high ground, even in the face of a second, inept, amphibious landing in August. The outstanding Ottoman officer was Colonel Kemal (later awarded the name Atatürk—father of the Turks). When Bulgaria entered the war the railway line from Germany to Turkey was opened and heavy artillery and shells were shipped to the Peninsula. By January 1916, the Allies, led by a new British commander, Sir Charles Monro, had evacuated all of their troops safely, their only notable success in the campaign[9,12].

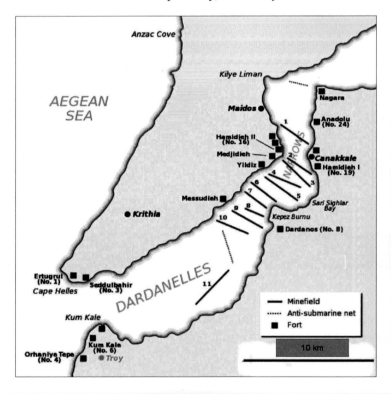

Shown on the map are the Ottoman forts and minefields.

20=

number of years the commander of the second British amphibious landing had served as Constable of the Tower of London before being sent to command the landing

3,689=

number of horses and mules taken safely off in the last stage in the British evacuation[12]

GALLIPOLI

Casualties at Gallipoli

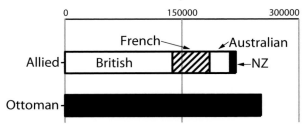

1.1 C.P. / 1 Allied

ITALY IN 1915

The Italians entered the war in May 1915, after signing a secret treaty in which the Allies promised them magnificent spoils. Their long border with Austro-Hungary was largely mountainous. They undertook a series of attacks along what is now the frontier with Slovenia[73], striking toward the river Isonzo, making little progress but sustaining terrible losses[9,20]. The heavy interrupted line shows the border between Italy and Austro-Hungary. The Italians proposed to take the city of Trieste.

LOSSES IN ITALY IN 1915

Casualties in Italy in 1915

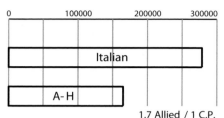

The Austro-Hungarians did better against the Italians than against the Russians[9].

1.7 Allied / 1 C.P.

PREPARING FOR A LONG WAR

Annual classes of Frenchmen for military service

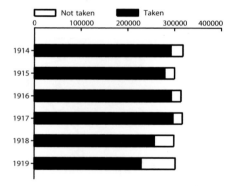

French recruits from colonies (in thousands)

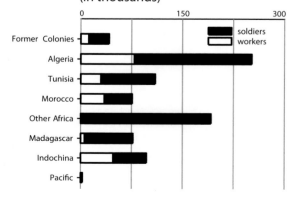

The political leaders now knew that they faced a long, bloody war. Future manpower was critical. They counted the number of their youths who would become eligible for military service, and, like the French shown in the graph, lowered their standards to take almost all[5]. They could also count their enemy's manpower, which led them to contemplate winning by bleeding their opponents white—attrition. The Allies also enlisted men from their overseas possessions, many of whom were used as assault troops[10].

500,000=

number of French soldiers reassigned to industry by end of year 1915[52]

EXPANDING THE BRITISH ARMY

The British were bolstered by men from their overseas territories. Canadians, Australians, and New Zealanders were used as elite storm troops, which accounts for the high percentage of casualties they suffered[9,10].

British overseas contingents from:

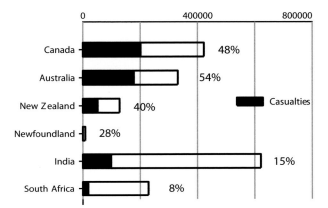

The British expanded their small army enormously, first by enlistment and then by conscription. Initially most men went to the infantry[10]. Later the growth of the infantry slowed while the other branches continued to expand rapidly. The fraction of men in the artillery more than tripled (**4% to 14%**), but the increase in engineers was modest (**5% to 7%**)[9,10]. By 1918 there was a serious shortage of infantry replacements (page 80).

The most spectacular growth was in the number of men in the flying corps, which during the war became the Royal Air Force (RAF)[9,21]. Surprisingly the number of men assigned to the War Office in London (not shown) decreased initially and even at the end was only **110%** of its pre-war size.

Number of men in British Army

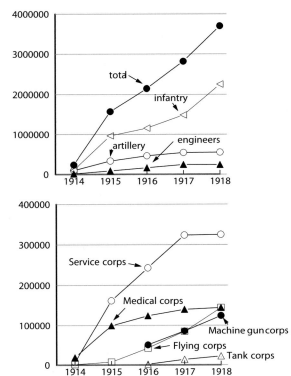

THE BRITISH ARTILLERY

British guns in France

The increase in the numbers of artillery men was matched by the increase in numbers of cannons. During the last two years of the war the total number of shells fired did not increase markedly, because each gun was fired less often[10].

NAVAL EXPANSION

Both sides continued to build more warships[9]. The Germans should have put all of their resources into submarines; they never had as many U-boats as they could have employed effectively.

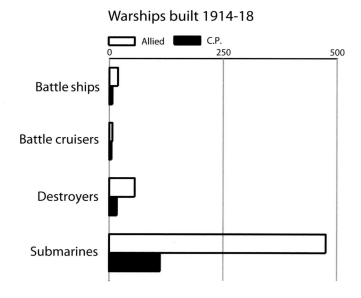

During the war the Germans used **635,000** tons of barbed wire, **600 million** sandbags, and **160 million** firework signals for communication from the front[29]—enough wire to be wrapped around the circumference of the earth **130 times**. The rate of production of trench supplies increased notably in the first years of the war, reached an asymptote, and then decreased[9].

GERMAN WIRE AND CANNONS

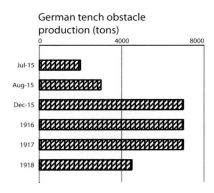

German tench obstacle production (tons)

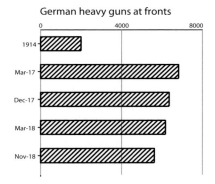

German heavy guns at fronts

The Germans increased their supply of heavy guns, and by 1917 had reached the level they thought necessary[9]. The number of mortars was increased even more[9].

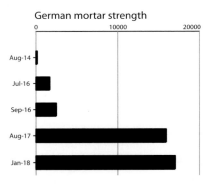

German mortar strength

THE WESTERN FRONT IN 1916

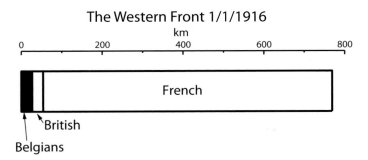

The Western Front 1/1/1916

km

French

British

Belgians

The French still held the bulk of the line, but the British contribution expanded markedly during 1916 as they continued to bring over the men enlisted in the first months of the war[9,10].

VERDUN

Falkenhayn counted the number of French youths and decided that he could knock France out of the war by using the superior German heavy artillery to destroy the Frenchmen defending the fortress city of Verdun. Verdun was vulnerable because the railway line running into the city had been cut in 1914. The German infantry was supposed to advance only when the defenders were dead or had abandoned their trenches. The army commander, the Imperial Crown Prince, was set on taking the city. Soon the German infantry attacked positions from which French survivors fought fiercely. General Henri Pétain was given command of the French front. He supplied and reinforced the defenders by truck. Both sides suffered terribly; the French front bent but was not penetrated[73]. Overall, the Germans lost almost as many men as the French; a total failure for Falkenhayn, whose intelligence staff kept assuring him that French losses far exceeded German[9].

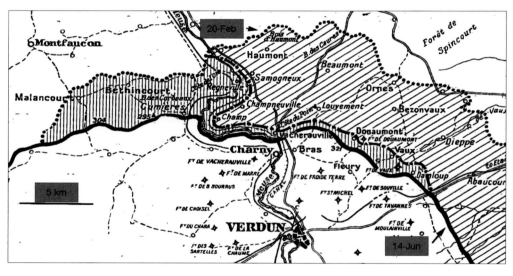

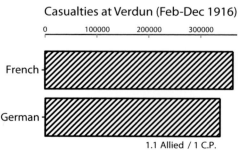

Casualties at Verdun (Feb-Dec 1916)

1.1 Allied / 1 C.P.

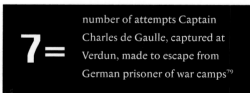

7 = number of attempts Captain Charles de Gaulle, captured at Verdun, made to escape from German prisoner of war camps[79]

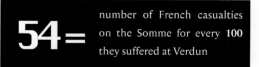

54 = number of French casualties on the Somme for every **100** they suffered at Verdun

THE BATTLE OF THE SOMME

On 1 July the British and French attacked in the valley of the Somme, after days of heavy bombardment that failed to eliminate the defenders or to cut much of the German barbed wire. The French made minor progress, the British even less, and both sides suffered terrible losses[48]. Gradually the British adopted rehearsed attacks with limited objectives, which made it more difficult for their enemy. The battle continued until stopped by bad weather in the autumn.

30 kg=

weight of equipment carried by a British infantryman in the initial Somme attack[63]

Number of men in an engagement in the Somme July 1, 1916

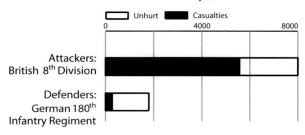

3.2 kph=

pace that the British infantry was ordered to advance toward the enemy tranches in the initial Somme attack[63]

13=

number of separate trenches encountered wherever a line was drawn through a map of the German fortifications on the Somme

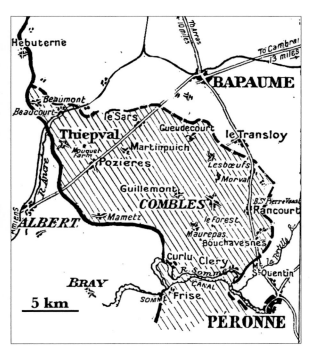

The hatched area shows the British gains in 1916[73].

1916 CASUALTIES IN THE WEST

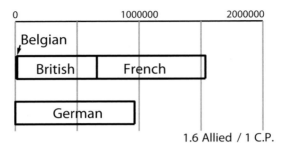

Casualties in the West 1916

1.6 Allied / 1 C.P.

THE WAR AT SEA

The navies had relatively few men and their casualties were comparatively light[10,33]. Early in the war the British lost to the German Asiatic Fleet off Chile, but then destroyed their opponents near the Falkland Islands. They made a successful cruiser foray against the German offshore screen at the Dogger Bank. The German battle cruisers bombarded fortified English seaports, killing civilians, as an unsuccessful ruse to draw part of the British fleet into an ambush. The great meeting of the fleets was at Jutland in 1916. British losses were slightly higher, but the German High Seas Fleet never ventured far out thereafter: the British navy maintained the blockade, the German navy deterred Allied amphibious landings on the continent.

Number of seamen British Navy had:

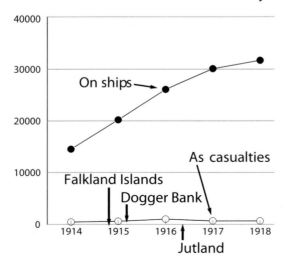

ITALY IN 1916

The Italians continued to launch attacks along the Isonzo River[20] (map page 41). Losses were heavy; gains were modest[9]. In the summer the Austro-Hungarians attacked southward through the mountains from the Tyrol, into the Trentino[9]. After a promising start, many of the attackers had to be transferred back to the Russian front (page 50) and to Romania (page 51) and the advance stalled. The breakthrough in Italy, at Caporetto, came in the following year.

Distances for Italy (km)

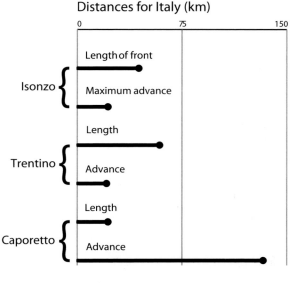

Casualties at Trentino

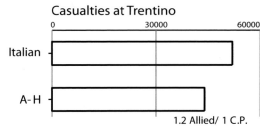

1.2 Allied/ 1 C.P.

TOTAL CASUALTIES IN ITALY IN 1916

Casualties in Italy 1916

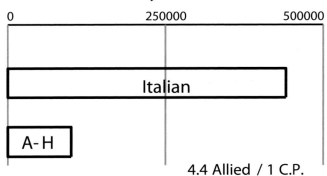

4.4 Allied / 1 C.P.

THE EAST IN 1916

To draw Germans away from Verdun, the Russians attacked at Lake Naroch (in present-day Belarus). They assembled overwhelming superiority in troops and guns and attacked in March—they were defeated badly[9].

Lake Naroch March 1916

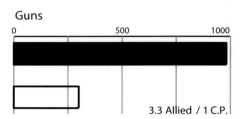

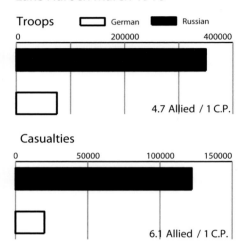

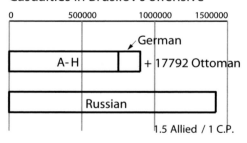

To help the Italians in the Tyrol, in June the Russian army group commanded by General Aleksey Brusilov attacked the Austro-Hungarian lines in what is now the Ukraine. The Austro-Hungarians thought their positions impregnable. Each of Brusilov's armies prepared assault trenches and dug tunnels, known as 'Russian saps', under their own wire, so it would not have to be cut before the attack. The Austro-Hungarians could not predict where the main thrust would be launched. The Russian spearhead broke through the Austro-Hungarian trench lines, taking **417,000** prisoners[13]. The advance stalled when they were far from their railheads and the front was stabilized by German reinforcements and Austro-Hungarians moved back from Italy[73]. The Russian strategic plan was that their other army groups would attack on the German front once the reserves had been sent south—but these attacks were never launched because Brusilov's losses were so heavy.

BRUSILOV'S OFFENSIVE

The front-line in the East at the beginning of 1916. The hatched area shows the ground gained by Brusilov's armies during the summer[73].

581 =

number of Austro-Hungarian guns captured by Brusilov's offensive[13]

In August the Romanians entered the war, adding **500,000** trained men to the Allied side. Falkenhayn had promised the Kaiser that they would remain neutral. Moreover, Falkenhayn's staff, dismayed by Verdun and by his rigid defensive tactics on the Somme, let their disapproval be known. He was replaced by Hindenburg and Ludendorff, who also became the supreme commanders of all of the armies of the Central Powers.

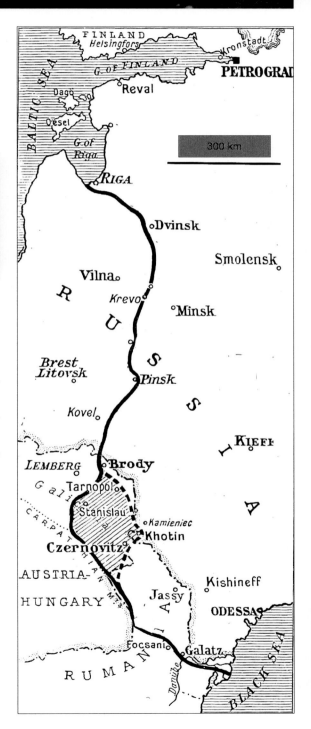

THE FALL OF ROMANIA

Hindenburg and Ludendorff promptly organized a two pronged invasion of Romania: through the mountains of Transylvania by a force commanded by Falkenhayn, and north from Bulgaria by an army commanded by Mackensen. In December the two armies entered Bucharest, and then drove further north. Romanian casualties were about **350,000** and German about **60,000**, but the Austro-Hungarian and Bulgarian numbers are uncertain[53].

The arrows show the direction of the attacks by the Central Powers, who went on to occupy all of the country except for the north around Jassy (now Iasi)[73]. The only Allied success was that a small sabotage team destroyed many of the Romanian oil fields.

CASUALTIES IN THE EAST IN 1916

107= days between the Romanian declaration of war and the entry into Bucharest of the armies of the Central Powers

Once again the Central Powers dominated in the East[9].

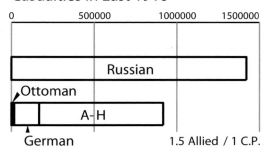

Casualties in East 1916

Russian
Ottoman
A-H
German
1.5 Allied / 1 C.P.

52 sq km= area of Romanian oilfields put out of action by a British sabotage team before the Germans arrived[90]

THE MIDDLE EAST IN 1916

The Ottomans battled the Russians in the Armenian lands in the Caucasus Mountains and the British in what is now Iraq and Palestine. They also sent some of their best divisions to help on the Eastern Front[9].

Casualties in Armenia 1916

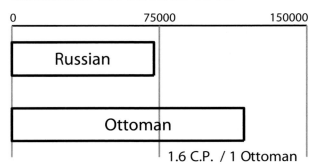

Russian
Ottoman
1.6 C.P. / 1 Ottoman

CASUALTIES IN THE MIDDLE EAST IN 1916

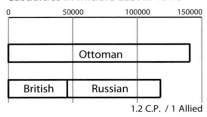

Casualties in Middle East in 1916

1.2 C.P. / 1 Allied

AFRICA IN 1916

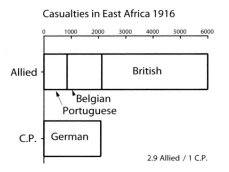

Casualties in East Africa 1916

2.9 Allied / 1 C.P.

The only remaining German enclave was East Africa. The Allies, led by the former Boer general Smuts, invaded by land and sea. The Germans, led by Lettow-Vorbeck, bloodied the invaders, and slipped away from their encirclement attempts[81].

IMPROVING WEAPONS

Both sides worked intensively to improve their arsenals. The Germans had **2000 scientists** and technicians working in their gas warfare program; the British about **1500**[38]. The gases used first, chlorine and phosgene, destroyed lung tissues when inhaled. In 1916 the Germans introduced mustard gas, which burned exposed skin and caused temporary blindness. Both sides now released more gas from missiles than from cylinders. The Germans developed combination

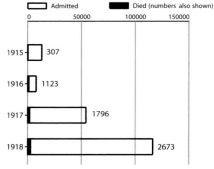

British hospitalized for gas poisoning

high explosive and gas shells, so those targeted would not know that gas was released. Protection against inhalation gases was simple in principle—they could be excluded by breathing though a cloth soaked in urine or through filters built into gas masks. Gas sent many into hospital, but the death rate was low[17]. It was a relatively humane weapon.

IMPROVEMENTS IN ARTILLERY

High explosive shells that were designed to detonate on impact often buried themselves in the mud, either not exploding or having their destructive power smothered. Super-sensitive impact fuses, like the British 106, were devised in time to cope with the slimy mud of Flanders in 1917[15].

Surveyors determined the precise location of every battery position and equipped them with aiming stakes pointing toward a set bearing, making it possible to fire accurately at coordinates on a map. The muzzle velocity of shells fired by each gun was determined on a test range, which further improved accurate firing by map[62].

Both sides developed techniques to draw accurate maps of the battlefields from aerial photographs and used flash-spotting to locate enemy artillery pieces[62]. The British developed the best sound-ranging apparatus, with microphones that could record the low frequency thud of heavy guns[22]. Six of these microphones were positioned along a length of front. When a gun fired the time taken for the sound to reach each microphone depended on the distance between the gun and the microphone. The responses of the microphones were recorded on moving photographic paper. The time differences between when the sound reached each microphone determined the position of the gun. The Americans adopted the British method.

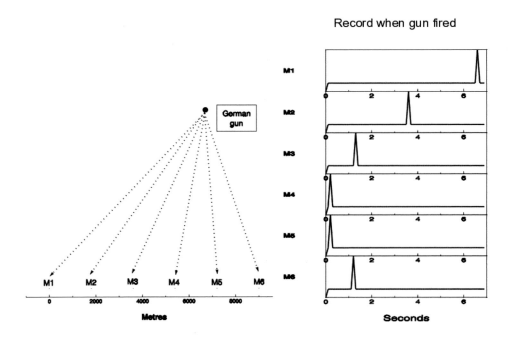

ARTILLERY SHELL PRODUCTION

Enormous numbers of shells were fired, so production was high priority for all of the combatants. Trench warfare revived grenades, thrown by hand or catapulted or fired from a rifle with a blank cartridge[10]. The Germans used **270 million** of them[29], their soldiers were trained to hurl volleys at attackers. The Russians had expanded shell production markedly by 1916[13], but the numbers they made in a year would only have supplied the British for two or three weeks when they were firing preparatory bombardments for an attack[10].

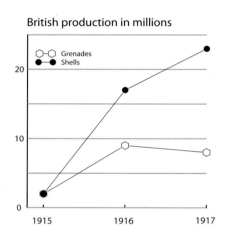

British production in millions

Russian supply of 6-inch shells

52% of the British shells were fired by 18-pdr field guns; most of the rest were fired by heavier guns, including those mounted on railway cars. The production of artillery pieces was speeded up and facilities were established to repair damaged and defective guns[10]. The percentage of shrapnel shells fired decreased.

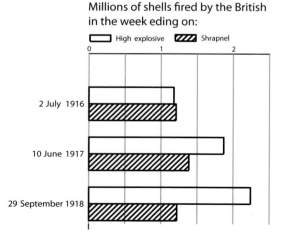

Millions of shells fired by the British in the week eding on:

LOCOMOTIVES AND GUN REPAIR

Toward the end of the Somme battle the British were unable to keep their troops at the front properly supplied. They relied on the overstretched French railway system. A civilian railway expert, Eric Geddes, was sent to France; he brought over locomotives and railwaymen and sorted out the problems[59]. Light railways were used for transportation close to the front, but they were good targets for the enemy artillery. Motor transport was less liable to disruption, and all of the belligerents increased production[10].

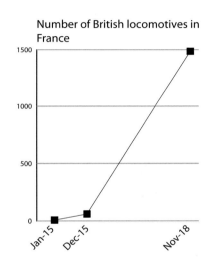

Number of British locomotives in France

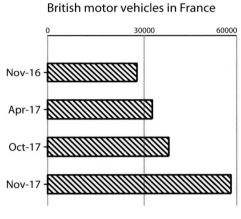

British motor vehicles in France

Number of British guns

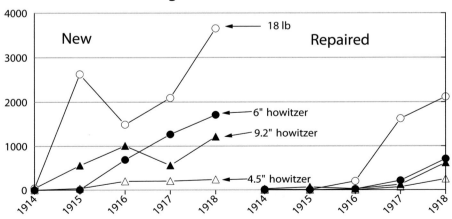

WORKERS AND THEIR PRODUCTS

German industrial production

Both sides at the outset took too many skilled workers into their armies, banking on the short war almost everyone predicted. Industrial production fell substantially and men had to be returned to the factories. Later the production of goods for war increased, but the production of civilian goods declined throughout the war[10,23].

700,000 =

number of Belgian men deported to work in Germany

Millions of items delivered to British troops

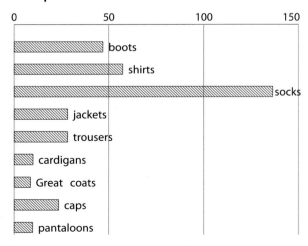

Along with the weapons and food, the troops required enormous quantities of clothing[10] and other items also needed by civilians.

17,000 =

number of French companies making armaments

THE FALL IN COAL AND STEEL PRODUCTION

Due to the shortage of workers, and later because some of them did not have enough food to work hard, German production of basics like steel and coal declined and failed to recover during the war[10]. The British managed to increase steel production during the war, but not coal production. During the winters homes were unheated, which was an additional trial for the millions of urban dwellers who did not have enough to eat and burned up precious calories by shivering.

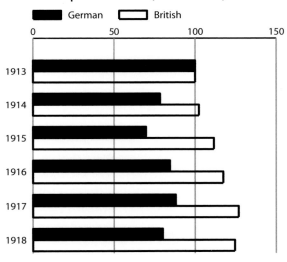

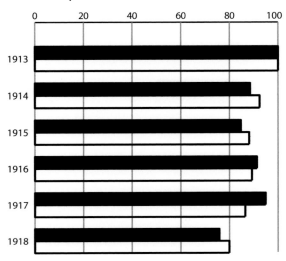

INCREASING ARMS PRODUCTION

When the Germans occupied the north of France the French lost **83%** of their iron ore production and **60%** of their steel[52]. The French immediately began to draw on every resource to maintain and expand war production. In Britain production increased greatly after the Ministry of Munitions[10, 80] was set up in 1915, directed by David Lloyd George. It had the power to tell people where they must work. Germany adopted the Hindenburg Plan in late 1916, which attempted to mobilize the entire country for the war effort[23]. They also forced Belgians to work in Germany. In Britain strikes were broken by threats of military service. In Germany labour activists were sent to the front, where they continued to agitate against the war (page 84). The Austro-German attack in Italy in autumn 1917 (page 74) hit trenches defended apathetically by industrial workers who had been drafted for going on strike[20].

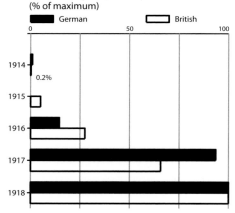

Machine gun production
(% of maximum)

The machine gun was one of the key weapons, and production was increased right up to the end of the war, especially of lighter guns, like the British Lewis, that could be brought forward in an attack.

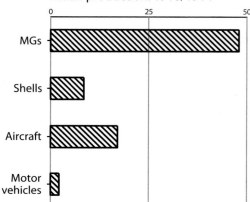

Italian production: 1918/1914

The Italians made enormous efforts to make goods for war[9]. They obtained additional necessaries and funds from their allies.

RUSSIAN SMALL ARMS PRODUCTION

After a lag the Russians also increased their stock of machine guns[13]. They started the war with a substantial supply of rifles, and added more from their own production and with imports[13]. But they had so many troops that some Russian infantrymen were sent into battle without rifles, instructed to take arms from the dead and wounded; a shameless statement of the worth placed on their lives. Many Russian rifles were captured or destroyed at the front. By 1917 the Russian army had fewer rifles than at the outset.

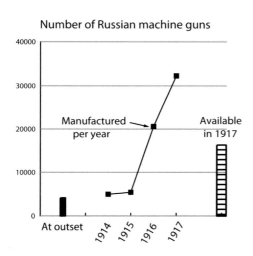

Number of Russian machine guns

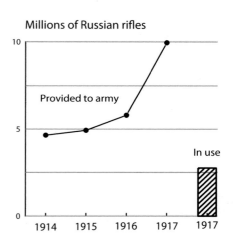

Millions of Russian rifles

Shells were also a problem for the Russians. Like the other belligerents, their peacetime stock was too low and there was an appreciable lag before they could increase production. Their foreign suppliers also needed time to adapt their factories to munitions[13].

Russian supply of 6-inch shells

4,000,000 = tons of iron ore imported to Germany from Sweden in 1915[70]

AEROPLANES

Aeroplanes produced per year

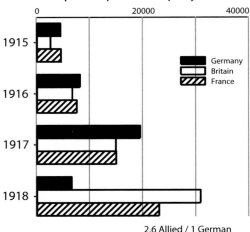

2.6 Allied / 1 German

There were spectacular increases in the production of newly emerging weapons, like the aeroplane[9,10,21]. The three major producers are shown in the graph. During the war the Allies made **117,158 planes** and the Central Powers made **43,946**[21]. German production fell in 1918 because of shortages of raw materials due to the blockade. The Americans usually flew French aeroplanes.

Major goals for aeroplane design were to increase speed and to climb higher[21].

Type	BHP	Top speed (mph)	Hours aloft	Top altitude
Bristol Scout 1914	84	86.5	2.5	15500'
Sopwith Pup 1916	84	104	3	17500'
Sopwith Camel 1917	150	115	2.5	20000'
Sopwith Dolphin 1918	210	128	2.25	21000'

The British invented the tank, which is still known by its original code name[9,48]. The French also produced many tanks. They were designed to smash down enemy barbed wire entanglements. The Germans built few tanks, they considered them too slow to be decisive weapons; for their offensive tactics they only needed to cut narrow lanes through the enemy wire. Therefore they used their limited resources to make motor lorries[78].

10,312= number of church bells from Prussian churches melted down for arms[70]

TANKS

Tank development stressed increases in speed and range[24,25], but headway in both tank and plane performance was stymied by difficulties in increasing the power of internal combustion engines. The French introduced smaller, somewhat faster tanks with guns in a swivelling turret.

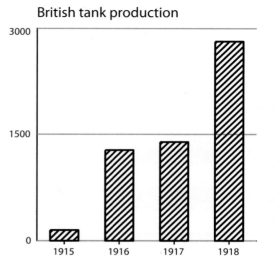

British tank production

Model	Crew	Weight (tons)	Speed (kph)	Range (km)	HP
Mark I	8	28	6	27	105
Mark IV	8	28	6	56	105
Mark VII	8	33	7.2	56	150
Medium A	4	14	13.4	128	90

CIVILIAN DEATHS AND
THE BLOCKADE OF BRITAIN

Deaths per thousand residents of Petrograd

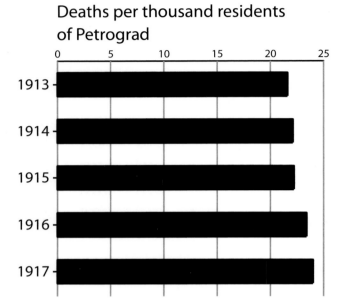

Civilian death rates in many cities increased during the war: inadequate nutrition, lack of soap for washing and cleaning, and cold increased illness and fatalities. The very young and the elderly were especially at risk. Petrograd (today St Petersberg) is shown because the privations and the increase in deaths there led to revolution[55]. At first glance the increase seems small, but by 1917 the war had caused more than **23,000** excess civilian deaths in the city.

In January 1917 the Germans declared that they would sink without warning any ships in the waters around the British Isles or those in the Mediterranean that were outside of designated shipping lanes for neutral vessels[73]. The German navy was confident that they would force the British to surrender by the end of the year. They also promised that if the US entered the war none of their troops would reach Europe. The US entered the war in April.

The triggerman. **Gavrilo Princip** (1894-1918) was a Serb from Bosnia-Herzegovina, which the Austro-Hungarians had taken from the Ottomans in 1878[85]. Then as now, the region also contained Moslems and Croats. The terrorists wanted the Bosnian Serbs incorporated into Serbia. In Belgrade, a Serbian intelligence officer, Major Dimitrijević (1876-1917), provided an automatic pistol and grenades, and smuggled them across the border. The police arrested 25 suspects; 10 were acquitted. Princip received the maximum sentence for a killer under age twenty—20 years. Three older men were executed. Princip died in prison from tuberculosis and malnutrition; in 1918 many prisoners starved because the ration was so meagre. Dimitrijević was executed for treason after a secret trial, while serving with the Serbian army in Salonica [84].

Hohenzollern and Habsburg. **William II**, German Kaiser and King of Prussia (1859-1941) [left] and **Archduke Franz Ferdinand** (1863-1914) [right] in the garden of the Archduke's castle at Konopischt (now in the Czech Republic) [85]. It was a fortnight before the murders. The Kaiser's left arm was withered by a birth injury. They became friends when the Kaiser supported the Archduke's marriage to an obscure Czech countess, defying Habsburg family law. The Archduke was planning a federal system to share political power with the restless minorities in the Empire.

The Karadjordjevićs. **King Peter of Serbia** (1844-1921) [left]. He came to power in 1903, after 45 years in exile, when the reigning king and his wife were murdered by a cabal of officers that included Dimitrijević. Peter led the country during the First Balkan War (1912-13) against the Ottoman Empire, and the Second Balkan War (1913) against the Bulgarians—allies in the first. In June 1914 he was forced to abdicate in favour of his son **Alexander** (1888-1934) [right] who became Prince Regent. In November 1918 Peter was made king of the new entity, Yugoslavia. He immediately gave his son all responsibility. Alexander became king when his father died and was assassinated in 1934 by a Croatian terrorist.

The Emperor of Austria and King of Hungary and Bohemia, **Franz Joseph** (1830-1916) [left]. He had barely survived a knife attack, his son committed suicide, his wife was killed by a terrorist, and his brother was shot by a Mexican firing squad. The old man wanted the Serbians punished for the murder of his nephew the Archduke, but signed the declaration of war only after being told falsely that Serbian artillery was bombarding Austria. Tsar **Nicholas II** of Russia (1868-1918) [right], talking to a tall British general. The Tsar was an erratic, intellectually limited and indecisive autocrat. In 1915 he took command of the Army. The Kaiser, King George V of Great Britain, and the Tsar were cousins.

Kaiser **Wilhelm II** as he liked to be seen [left]. He had that dangerous combination of intelligence and foolishness. A foreign diplomat aptly observed, 'In this highly organized nation, when you have ascended to the very top story you find not only confusion but chaos.' In exile he maintained that the war was a long planned British plot to destroy Germany. **Raymond Poincaré** (1860-1934) was president of France from 1913-1920 [right]. A firm supporter of the alliance with Russia, after the assassinations he visited the Tsar to demonstrate support. During the war his home was behind German lines. He deplored the Versailles Treaty as too lenient. After he left the presidency, he was prime minister four times.

Four of the leading members of the British Cabinet in 1913: **Winston Spencer Churchill** (1874-1965) the first lord of the admiralty [left]; Margot Asquith (1864-1926) [second from left]; **Herbert Henry Asquith** (1852-1926) the prime minister [third from left]; **David Lloyd George** (1863-1945) the chancellor of the exchequer [second from right]; and **Sir Edward Grey** (1862-1933) the foreign secretary [right]. The invasion of Belgium saved Grey from having to reveal the understandings with the French. He left office in 1916. The four politicians were enjoying a summer cruise on the admiralty yacht, which the prime minister used so that he could keep in contact with London by wireless.

Two kings who choose war. **Tsar Ferdinand of Bulgaria** (1861-1948) [left], a member of a princely family related to monarchs, was elected Prince Regent of Bulgaria in 1887, when he was a lieutenant in the Austro-Hungarian army. He became Tsar in 1908 after he proclaimed Bulgaria independent of the Ottoman Empire. He gained territory in the First Balkan War and lost it in the Second. In 1915 the Central Powers brought Bulgaria into the war with promises of lands from Macedonia, Greece, and Romania. He abdicated in October 1918 in favour of his son. His cousin **King Albert I of the Belgians** (1875-1934) [right] was the second son of the Count of Flanders and his Hohenzollern wife. At age 16 he unexpectedly was named heir to the Belgian throne, and became king in 1909. Albert refused to allow the German army to pass through Belgium, believing that his army and forts could stem the German advance until French and British reinforcements arrived. He spent the war years with the remains of his army in a tiny strip of unoccupied Belgium along the Channel coast. A dedicated mountaineer, he was killed climbing.

King Ferdinand of Romania (1865-1927) [left] carefully weighed the offers from the two sides. He opted for the Allies after the success of Brusilov's offensive in 1916 and was soon driven out of most of his nation, which he recovered and enlarged at Versailles. Born a prince of Hohenzollern-Sigmaringen, he was adopted by his childless uncle, King Carol I of Romania. His wife was a cousin of Tsar Nicholas. **Enver Pasha** (1881-1922) [right] was the Ottoman minister of war and one of a triumvirate of 'young Turks' who ruled the country. Sultan Mehmed V (1844-1918) was almost powerless. Enver led the Ottomans into the war and lost many men battling in the Caucasus. At the end of the war he became an exile and died fighting Russians in Central Asia. The other two members of the triumvirate were assassinated by Armenians revenging the massacres.

Greek antagonists. King **Constantine II** (1868-1923) [left] was the eldest son of King George I, who began life as a Danish prince and married a Russian. Constantine was educated in Greek and German universities and received further military education in Germany. He commanded the Greek armies defeated in the Greco-Turkish war (1897) and victorious in the First Balkan War (1912). His father was assassinated in 1913. As king, Constantine was victorious in the Second Balkan War (1913). In 1914 he hoped to keep Greece out of the war. His power was undermined by the Allied occupation of Salonica and later by their threat to bombard Athens. He abdicated in favour of his son in 1917. His son died in 1920 and a plebiscite restored Constantine to the throne. He abdicated again in 1922 after the Turks drove the Greeks out of Anatolia. **Eleftherios Venizelos** (1864-1936) [right] was a charismatic politician. Born in Ottoman Crete, he led the struggle that brought unification with Greece in 1908. In 1910 he became prime minister of Greece. He wanted to take in all of the land in which Greeks were under Ottoman rule, so he manoeuvred to join the Allies. When the Turks won the Ottoman Greeks became refuges.

The first two German commanders. **Helmut von Moltke** (1848-1916) [left] became chief of staff in 1906. (His uncle was the great general who defeated the Austrians in 1866 and the French in 1870.) He weakened the crucial right wing in Schlieffen's plan and then weakened it further by transferring troops to the Eastern Front. He approved the order for the German right wing to retire from the Marne, abandoning German hope for a swift victory. After six weeks of war he was replaced by **Erich von Falkenhayn** (1861-1922) [right] the Prussian minister of war. Falkenhayn attacked futilely with untrained recruits in Flanders, botched the introduction of poison gas, launched the failed attack on Verdun, and demanded rigid defensive tactics in the Somme. After he was replaced he led armies in Romania, Iraq, and Palestine.

The first two French commanders. **Joseph Joffre** (1852-1931) [left] was a military engineer who became commander in 1911. True to French military doctrine that attack wins, he started the war by hurling his troops forward in extemporized attacks. Casualties were enormous. He shifted to the defensive, withdrawing his left wing before the German advance and reinforcing them. The attack along the Marne and from Paris stopped the German incursion. In 1915 and 1916 his attacks to drive the Germans from French soil were bloody failures. At the end of 1916 he was made Marshal of France and replaced by **Robert Nivelle** (1856-1924) [right]. An artillery officer, he recaptured much of the ground lost at Verdun by a surprise attack, in which the infantry advanced behind a creeping artillery barrage. He was confident that he could break through the enemy line. He spoke excellent English, and his elevation was strongly supported by Lloyd George. His attack on the Chemin des Dames was a disaster. Replaced in May 1917, he was transferred to North Africa.

The two BEF Commanders. Sir **John French** (1852-1925) [left] was a cavalry commander in the Boer War. He led the BEF to France. Defeated at Mons, he decided to retreat to the channel coast, but Kitchener ordered him to join in the French counter-attack at the Marne. In 1915 he twice failed to break through the German lines, for which he blamed a shortage of artillery ammunition. After he was replaced he commanded the Home Forces and then became Lord Lieutenant of Ireland. He was replaced in the BEF by Sir **Douglas Haig** (1861-1928) [right], another cavalryman. He led the British attacks on the Somme and at Passchendaele. In 1918 he held his army together during the German breakthroughs and then pressed the withdrawing enemy until they collapsed.

Henri-Philippe Pétain (1856-1951) [left] was about to retire when the war came. He understood how to coordinate artillery with infantry and how to use aeroplanes; he led several successful attacks. When the Germans seemed about to take Verdun, he was given command there. He kept supplies flowing up the single road into the city and relieved troops before they lost their ability to fight. He refused to counter-attack to recover lost ground, so after the city was saved he was moved elsewhere. When given command of the army Nivelle had almost destroyed, he restored morale and cohesion, but again attacked only when sure that casualties would be moderate. His defensive tactics blunted the last German efforts to take Paris in 1918. **John Pershing** (1860-1948) [right] fought Native Americans and Spaniards in Cuba, before leading a punitive expedition into Mexico. In France he abided by Wilson's order to build an American army, which went into action in 1918.

The opponents in Italy. **Luigi Cadorna** (1850-1928) [left] became commander of the Italian Army in 1914. He was an able administrator who stayed well behind the front. He threw his army into eleven attacks across difficult terrain against a skilful enemy. Then the Austro-Germans broke through at Caporetto and almost destroyed his army. He was replaced. **Svetozar Boroević** (1856-1920) [right] was a Serb who rose from corporal to corps commander in the Austro-Hungarian Army. Early in the war he was effective in Poland, so he was given command of the Isonzo front. After Caporetto, the Austro-Hungarian advance was halted at the Piave River. He was ordered to attack that line in 1918, but the attack failed. When his army and country fell apart, he marched his remaining troops back to Austria. His offer to serve the new Yugoslavia was rejected.

The team that replaced Falkenhayn. **Paul von Hindenburg** (1847-1934) [left] and **Erich Ludendorff** (1865-1937) [right] both were educated in military schools, won admission to the Staff College by highly competitive examinations, and then served terms on the General Staff. Hindenburg was wounded in the war with Austria, was a hero in the Franco-German war, and became a corps commander. He retired in 1911. While on the Staff, Ludendorff planned an infiltration attack to capture the vital railway bridges in the Belgian city of Liege. He accompanied the assault force as an observer, took over when its commander was killed, and captured the city. When two Russian armies invaded East Prussia, Hindenburg was given command of the defending army with Ludendorff as chief of staff. They met for the first time on the train east. They surrounded and destroyed one Russian army and then drove the second off. They would agree on a plan, and then the energetic, meticulous Ludendorff had the scores of orders written. Hindenburg met with front-line officers to listen to their problems and ideas. They used elastic defences and developed the tactics to break through trench lines. They eliminated moderate politicians by threatening to resign and failed to recognize when further attacks became futile, blocking any hope for a negotiated peace.

Two eminent Russian soldiers. **Grand Duke Nicholas** (1856-1929) [left] was appointed commander in 1914; he had seen action only in the Russian-Turkish War of 1887. Hindenburg thought him a formidable adversary who was handcuffed by the Russian's sclerotic command structure. After the great Austro-German victories he was replaced by the Tsar in August 1915. He became governor-general in the Caucasus, where the Russian army was successful. He went into exile in 1919, and took no part in the Russian civil war. **Alexi Brusilov** (1853-1926) [right] was the fourth generation in his family to serve as a Russian officer. He distinguished himself in the Russian-Turkish war, and then spent years at the Cavalry Officer School in St Petersburg. A superb horseman, he rose to command the school. He started the war as a successful Army commander. In March 1916, he was offered command of the army group on the south-west front, he accepted on the proviso that they would attack. He befuddled the Austro-Hungarians by attacking simultaneously at a number of locations and then exploited the most successful for the breakthrough. After the revolution he was appointed supreme commander. His determination to fight on to win the war led to his replacement. In 1920 he became a general in the Red Army.

Field guns. All of the armies had field guns much like the British 18-pounder [above]. They were mobile and devastated men in the open with the 375 lead shrapnel balls discharged by each shell. Arguably the best was the French 75 mm, which had a hydraulic system that took the recoil and returned the gun almost precisely to its initial position, so it did not require re-training. The Americans bought French guns, rather than trying to develop their own. Guns like the Russian light howitzer [below] were better suited for trench warfare, especially when firing high explosive shells.

Howitzers. The Central Powers were prepared to take heavy guns onto the field, like this howitzer [left]. They usually fired high explosive shells. The bursting shells released a great plume of noxious black smoke, which made them even more terrifying. The British 8-in howitzer [below] reached the front in 1916. A shell is ready to be loaded.

New high muzzle velocity, long range guns were developed during the war, like these French 155 mm guns [above]. They are shown ready to be put into action for Nivelle's counter-attack at Verdun, in which they played a major role. By 1918 AA guns and their mountings had evolved markedly [below]. A high velocity, rapid firing gun that could fire almost straight up mounted on an all-terrain vehicle with caterpillar treads.

The most famous guns. A Krupp 42 cm howitzer [above], popularly known as 'Big Bertha'. Built secretly, they, and comparable Austro-Hungarian guns, demolished the French and Belgian frontier forts. Pictured below is one of the Krupp modified naval guns that bombarded Paris in 1918. Note the truss that kept the barrel straight. The recoil sent the gun backwards along the rail tracks. This gun is on a test range.

Much of the artillery fire was on targets the gunners could not see, so spotters were essential. Observers in the baskets hanging from kite balloons had magnificent views of the front and of the enemy rear area. They were selected for excellent map reading skills and strong stomachs because often the baskets bounced crazily. By 1916 the line of the front was marked by two strings of kite balloons. They were defended by anti-aircraft guns. If an attacker was spotted the observer would would parachute, as in the picture, while the balloon was winched down as rapidly as possible. If the attacker hit the balloon it would be become a fireball of burning hydrogen. Aviators were not provided with parachutes until the Germans issued them in 1918.

Shells and geology. The effects of shellfire depend on the landscape. In Flanders [above] the fields were just above the water line, and were drained by ditches dug and maintained for centuries by farmers. The shells destroyed the drainage and created a morass in which tanks could not move and in which men and animals might drown. Much of the Italian frontier along the Isonzo is mountainous. Between the mountains and the sea is a relatively flat limestone plateau, the Carso [below]. The rugged surface is difficult to walk over. Shells threw off rocks as deadly as their fragments. The Austro-Hungarians blasted out trenches and enlarged the natural caverns as shelters and for ammunition storage.

Other battlefields. The countryside in the Somme [above] is gently rolling, with cleared fields dotted with managed woods. The shellfire destroyed the woods and pockmarked the fields. When the autumn rains came the shell holes became ponds and it was impossible for men to keep dry. Much of the war in East Africa involved manoeuvring through jungle [below]. Most of the supplies were carried by men, so both sides employed large numbers of bearers.

Supplying Shells. The artillery war consumed shells by the millions [above] which none of the combatants had anticipated, so in 1915 both sides rationed shells to their artillery. Manufacturing expanded to meet the need. Pictured below is a British factory manufacturing fuses for shells. The United States sold shells to all of the Allies. At first, a significant number of the shells manufactured by new suppliers were duds.

Lloyd George, as Chancellor of the Exchequer. The shortage of shells created a political crisis in Britain. In response, the Government established a Ministry of Munitions headed by Lloyd George. The 'Welsh Wizard' recruited 'doers and pushers' from industry, who brought more factories into war production—output soared. When Field Marshal Kitchener drowned on his way to Russia, Lloyd George took his place at the War Office. At the end of 1916 he replaced Asquith as prime minister. He chaired a five man war committee. They waged total war, conscripting six million men, rationing food, pressing the navy to convoy, encouraging military campaigns in Palestine, Salonica, and Italy. At the end of 1918, the coalition government was returned to power in the 'khaki election', promising to squeeze the Germans 'until the pips squeak'. He manoeuvred adroitly to defend British interests at the Peace Conference. He fell from power in 1922 when the British had to withdraw their troops from Anatolia to avoid defeat by the Turkish nationalists.

Changes in leadership. **Georges Clemenceau** (1841-1929) [left] was a newspaper editor and politician, and was prime minister from 1906-1909. He refused cabinet positions in the early years of the war, criticising lack of commitment to total victory. In November 1917 he became prime minister—the fifth in that office during the war—and minister for war, promising 'war and nothing but war'. During the dark days of 1918, when the enemy seemed likely to take Paris, he retained power by 377 votes to 110 and had Foch appointed supreme allied commander. At the Peace Conference he fought implacably to make the Germans pay and for French occupation of the Rhineland and the coal-rich Saar Basin. In 1920, the National Assembly did not elect him President. The Emperor Franz Joseph died at age 86 in 1915 after reigning for 68 years. His successor, **Karl I** (1887-1922) [right], was his grandnephew. Karl was a devout Catholic who wanted to end the war. He forbade the Austro-Hungarian army to use poison gas. Secretly, even from his own ministers, he approached the French, supporting their claim to Alsace and Lorraine. His intermediary was his brother-in-law, an officer in the Belgian Army. In 1918 there were leaks about his negotiations and concessions. Karl swore they were untrue. Clemenceau published some of his letters. Completely besmirched, Karl had to toe the German line. When the Austrian Republic was proclaimed Karl fled to Switzerland. For the rest of his short life—he died of tuberculosis—he manoeuvred to regain a throne.

Theobald von Bethmann-Hollweg (1856-1921) [left] was German Imperial Chancellor from 1909-1917, appointed by the Kaiser. The times required a Bismarck, and he was no Bismarck. Before the war he was unable to moderate the naval construction race with Great Britain. When the Archduke was assassinated, he did not rescind the 'blank cheque' the impulsive Kaiser handed to the Austro-Hungarians. During the war, his moves to negotiate a peace came to nothing. He opposed unrestricted submarine warfare but bowed to military pressure. In the summer of 1917 the Reichstag passed a peace resolution, while Hindenburg and Ludendorff wanted him dismissed. Pressed from both sides, he resigned. **John Pierpont Morgan** (1837-1913) [right] created one of the most powerful American banks. An ardent anglophile, the bank became the conduit for Allied arms purchases in the United States and loaned large sums to the Allies. The JP Morgan bank continued in that role after his death; it would have been broken if the Allies were defeated.

The British battleship *Dreadnaught* [above]. Designed by an Admiralty committee led by Sir John Fisher and launched in 1906, it completely outclassed all other battleships by its heavy guns, massive armour, and the speed provided by steam turbines. The Germans immediately started building similar vessels. The picture reveals a design problem: the funnel placed immediately in front has blackened the superstructure. Its smoke often blocked the view of the gun layers, and heated the ladder-way within the tripod until it was impassable. The British battle cruiser squadron [below]. Both sides in the naval race were especially pleased with their battle cruisers. They had the guns and turbines of a battleship but less armour, so they were faster. The fight between the battle cruiser squadrons was the hottest action at Jutland. Here they are leaving port after the armistice.

Admirals. **John Arbuthnot Fisher** (1841-1920) [left] initiated the naval revolution with dreadnaughts and battle cruisers when he was first sea lord. In 1914 he was recalled from retirement by Winston Churchill. He agreed to try to force the Dardanelles with old battleships, but resigned when some were sunk, knowing that their skilled crews were needed to man vessels under construction. Churchill lost the Admiralty. **John Jellicoe** (1881-1970) [right] commanded the Grand Fleet at Jutland. The Germans were forced back into their harbours, but it was not the great victory the public expected. Jellicoe was promoted from the dashing commander of the battle cruisers to first sea lord. When the U-boats were unleashed on British shipping he resisted using convoys until forced to give way. At the end of 1917 he was dismissed as first sea lord and made an Earl.

Aerial battle. Dirigibles were important weapons in the early years of the war. A German Zeppelin over London is attacked by a British Farman, a 'pusher' in which the cockpits are in front of the propeller [above]. The dirigibles became death traps when the British invented a phosphorus bullet, which ignited the hydrogen that provided buoyancy. Below is a German monoplane that early in the war was the most successful fighter. It was designed by Antony Fokker (1890-1939), a Dutch engineer who also solved the problem of how to have a machine gun fire through a spinning propeller: the propeller shaft triggers the gun at the appropriate position.

Later Allied fighters. A British Sopwith [above], one of the series of successful models designed by the engineer Thomas Sopworth (1888-1989). A Spad VII [below], the first French fighter that used the synchronized mechanism to fire through the propeller. The Americans also flew Spads. There was a ceaseless race to produce better fighters. The Germans set up competitions for the manufacturers. Their competing models were judged at a fly-off, piloted by front-line aviators.

German fighters. The highly manoeuvrable Fokker triplane [above] was introduced to counter the Sopwith triplane. The Fokker dominated the western skies in 1917, especially those flown by von Richthoven's flying circus. They flew as a tightly controlled group, fighting when the odds were in their favour. Each plane was colour coded, so that the squadron leader always knew who was who. The Fokker D.VII [below] was introduced in 1918. They were so feared that the armistice specified that every D.VII must be turned over to the Allies. Fokker smuggled a train-load of them into the Netherlands, bribing the customs men with sewing machines for their wives.

Allied heavy bombers. Both sides developed large bombers with extended ranges. The Russians made some of the most impressive multi-engined planes [above]. Below is a British Handley-Page with folding wings for easier storage. The Germans were delivered an early model which landed at one of their aerodromes by a navigational mistake. In 1918 Winston Churchill, the minister of munitions, was building many of them to assault German cities from the air in 1919.

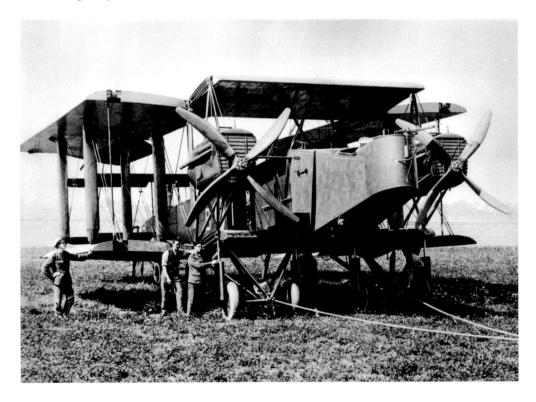

The largest Russian bomber [above]. It was never put into production. The civilian in the cockpit is the designer, Igor Sikorsky (1889-1972). Later, working in the United States, he pioneered in helicopter design. German Gotha bombers [below] attacked London in the last two years of the war. They flew at high altitude with the crew breathing oxygen and descended to bomb. They handled well when loaded with bombs, but poorly when empty. Most of their losses came at the end of the mission when they tried to land.

Arthur J. Balfour (1848-1930) [left] was British prime minister from 1902-1905. When Prime Minister Asquith formed the coalition in 1915, Balfour became first lord of the admiralty. The following year, when Lloyd George took power, Balfour became foreign secretary. **Chaim Weizmann** (1874-1952) [right] was a chemist at Manchester University who became director of Admiralty laboratories in 1916. He discovered how to make acetone, vital for the synthesis of cordite, by bacterial fermentation. Weizmann was one of Balfour's constituents and was also a prominent Zionist. He persuaded Balfour to issue his Declaration that Britain 'views with favour the establishment in Palestine of a national home for the Jewish people'. Weizmann was a founder of the Jewish University in Jeruselem and the first president of Israel.

Poison gas transformed the war. The Germans began in 1915 by releasing chlorine from cylinders, like the attack shown [left]. Cylinder release required a favourable wind and blowback was always a danger. It was better to release gas from artillery shells or from large canisters fired from specialized mortars. In 1917 the Germans introduced mustard gas, which blisters the skin. Some mustard gas casualties [right] had damage to the cornea of their eyes, like the Americans shown. The damp bandages alleviated the burning pain. Some patients became blind, but most recovered normal sight in a few weeks. Mustard gas lingers on the ground, so it was used to seal off parts of the battlefield. It took the Allies a year to produce their own mustard gas. One of the first German casualties was Corporal Adolph Hitler (1889-1945).

Gasmasks [above] filter out poisonous gases. Initially they were simple gauze pads or cloth helmets impregnated with chemicals. By 1918 they fitted tightly over the face; the German model is shown. The mask was sealed against the skin with rubber. By 1918 Germany did not have rubber for the seals, so newly-issued masks were ineffective. Every German knew about this problem—morale sank. Behind the lines the soldiers looked forward to payday [below], like the Germans shown on the Eastern Front.

Submarines were the pre-eminent naval weapon of the war. Above is a freighter torpedoed by the submarine in the foreground. German U-boats [below] took an enormous toll on Allied shipping. Here two meet at sea to exchange news. The most successful commanders became national heroes. When the Germans adopted unrestricted undersea warfare in 1917, their navy promised to take Britain out of the war that year, ignoring the possibility that their enemies would fight back effectively.

An artist's portrayal of the sinking of the *Lusitania* off the coast of Ireland in May 1915. A torpedo from U-20 killed **1,198** of the 1,959 pasengers, including children. The image of Germany suffered throughout the world. Added to the civilians killed in Belgium and stirred by skillful Allied propaganda, it gave a picture of ruthless indifference to human suffering. The foolish Kaiser had suggested to his troops going to put down the Boxer Rebellion in China that they should behave like Huns, and now the appelation stuck.

Barbed wire was a largely unanticipated weapon. Above, a French patrol creeps through a relatively modest entanglement near Verdun. Getting attackers through the wire was a challenge. The simplest method is to use wire cutters, like these Frenchmen [below]. This is impractical when the attackers advance as a line, intending to arrive at the enemy trench synchronously to deliver a bayonet attack. Therefore the Allies used prolonged bombardments to cut wire before their attacks on the Somme, often failing to make a breach. In 1918 the Germans largely relied on cutters, who made lanes for the attackers to snake though.

Tanks were another answer to wire. Above, a British tank crushes its way though an entanglement. They were first used in small numbers toward the end of the Battle of the Somme, revealing the secret and giving the enemy time to prepare countermeasures for the following year. Some of the French tanks [below] were smaller, faster, and had their guns in rotating turrets: protypes for the future. The disadvantage was their light armour. They were used in the counter-attack on the Marne in 1918 by the Americans as well. The Germans made few tanks, deciding that they were not effective enough to warrant using scarce resources[78].

The machine gun was one of the key weapons of the war. Pictured above is a Belgian machine gun detachment in action early in the war. The gun was pulled into position by a dog, used in Belgium to pull farm carts. The Germans used trained dogs to find wounded men on the battlefield, and both sides used them as messengers. Below, an Austro-Hungarian machine gun crew is in action against the Italians in the mountains along the Isonzo River.

Facing the machine guns. French infantry attacking in 1914 [above]. The French believed that the offensive fit their national character, so they began the war by hurling waves of infantry into the attack, with little artillery support, sustaining enormous losses. Below, Russian cavalry form for an attack. As the number of machine guns in action increased in the West, cavalry attacks became increasingly hazardous. In the East, where there were fewer machine guns and less field artillery, they were used throughout the war, in the Russian Civil War, and the Polish-Soviet War that followed.

Horse transport was essential. Above, a line of French wagons are bringing supplies to the front. When the Allies landed on Gallipoli, they also landed many animals [below]. Here we see the preparations for the withdrawal, during which many beasts were slaughtered to keep them out of enemy hands. The Americans brought thousands of mules to France; they are slower but carry heavier loads.

Battlefield conditions were formidable for both men and beasts; here British horses are struggling in French mud. Every nation had prepared to conscript horses if war came. By the end of the war the Central Powers were so short of horses that some infantry divisions were unable to relocate without special assistance. As the war went on lorries carried more and more of the material and also men [below]. French lorries saved Verdun and in 1918 they rapidly brought reserves to contain the German offensives.

Two notable commanders. **August von Mackensen** (1849-1945) [left] was a corps commander at Tannenberg in 1914 and led the breakthrough at Gorlice-Tarnow in 1915. Then he commanded the joint German, Austro-Hungarian, Bulgarian army that conquered Serbia and Montenegro. He also commanded the joint German, Bulgarian and Ottoman army that entered Romania from the south, crossed the Danube and occupied Bucharest. **Ferdinand Foch** (1851-1929) [right] was an influential military thinker, famously writing that 'the will to conquer is the first condition of victory.' He headed the Staff College from 1907-1911. He led an army in the Battle of the Marne and then commanded the French Army Group North, but after its terrible losses in the Somme he was sent to Italy. He was recalled as chief of staff when Pétain became commander, and then in March 1918 he was made Supreme Commander of the Allied Armies. He coordinated the Allied defences, and then kept relentless pressure on the withdrawing enemy until the armistice.

Two British assets. **Jan Christian Smuts** (1870-1950) [left], once a Boer general, led British armies in South-West and then in East Africa. In 1917 he became one of the five members of the British War Cabinet and was a leader in the establishment of the Royal Air Force. He signed the Versailles Treaty for South Africa, and also signed the treaty ending the second war with Germany. **John Norton Griffiths** (1871-1930) [right] was a flamboyant British engineer who fought in the Boer War and made a fortune building railways. In the Great War he built fortifcations on the Western Front and oversaw the digging of the mines that destroyed the German trenches on the Messines Ridge. Sent to Romania with his batman and a supply of gold, they destroyed many oilwells and oil stores before the Germans arrived[90].

Two almost forgotten movers and shakers. **Eric Geddes** [left] was a railway man brought to the Ministry of Munitions by Lloyd George. In a few months he vastly expanded shell output, but the shells piled up on French wharfs. He was sent to France to get the railways running. Haig made him a lieutenant general; he is wearing the uniform. In 1917 Lloyd George moved him to the Admiralty to get ships built; he was commisioned as a vice admiral. Next he became first lord, leading the successful fight against the U-boats. After the war he left politics and formed Imperial Airways. **Sir Charles Monro** (1860-1929) [right] commanded a corps and then an army in the BEF. He was given command in the Middle East in October 1915. After inspecting the toeholds on Gallipoli, he advised withdrawal. Churchill complained that he 'came, saw, and capitulated'. Lord Kitchener made a hurried inspection and agreed. The withdrawal was done in stages, without the loss of a single man. Monro ended the war as the Commander of the Indian Army in the Third Anglo-Afghan War (1919), in which the Afghans won the right to conduct their own affairs.

Two successful commanders. **Paul Emil von Lettow-Vorbeck** (1870-1964) [left] was a lieutenant colonel commanding 3,200 troops in German East Africa. Outnumbered, he adopted guerrilla tactics and foiled the Allies to the end. He returned home as a national hero. Armando Diaz (1961-1928) [right] was an Italian artillery officer who was made commander of the army after Caporreto in 1917. He held the Austro-Hungarians along the Piave River and restored his men's confidence. The following year they repulsed an attempt to cross the river, and then counter-attacked, capturing many prisoners as the Austro-Hungarian army fell apart.

Field fortifications. Initially the infantry fought from available ditches or simple trenches [above], like the Germans shown on the front near Warsaw in 1915 who are firing at an aeroplane. By 1917 German fortifications were largely concrete blockhouses [below], used for machine gun nests and command posts. Most of the infantry fought from shell holes instead of trenches, which were spotted too easily by enemy artillery observers. The Germans were working toward 'the invisible battlefield'.

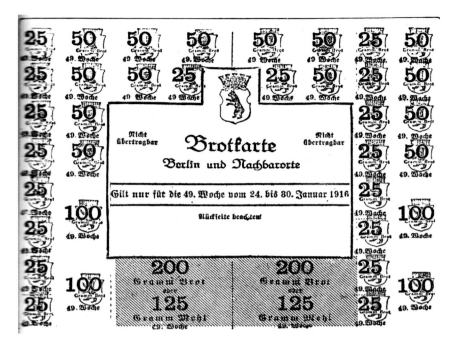

Food shortages. A German bread ration card [above]. Food became short for many people in urban areas in the Central Powers due to the blockade, bad weather, and maladroit administration. The rich and war workers still fed well, which created much resentment. Below, a queue of British shoppers wait to buy potatoes. The British imported food, which became short when the U-boats were let loose. Rationing was introduced. It was fair and created little resentment. Bread was never rationed, so no one went hungry, but its quality became very poor.

Millions of European children were malnourished. Pictured above is a feeding station for Viennese children. Vienna was especially hard hit because little food was grown in Austria and many regions hoping to leave the Empire resisted sending food to their overlords. The pitiable, starving child close to death [left] is a Russian. The swollen belly comes from a deficit of proteins in the blood.

Wounded. A wounded Canadian is helped toward the rear by a comrade who is also shepherding two German prisoners [above]. Below, wounded Austro-Hungarians lie in a field hospital set up in a church behind the Isonzo front. Straw was the customary bedding.

More wounded. A Russian field hospital [above] provided with religious consolation. The lightly wounded [below], like these cheery Britons, were given opiates to minimize pain and knew they were out of the front for a time at least.

Journey's end. A dead German soldier [above] and a German cemetery in France [below].

Turkish soldiers frozen to death fighting in the mountains [above]. Mutilated Germans [below].

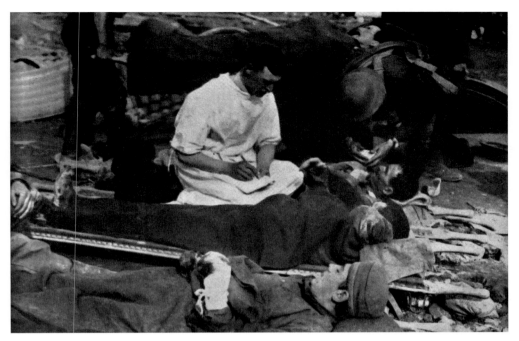

Medical care. Wounded were first collected at aid stations [above] where their names and numbers were recorded. Note the captured German in the foreground. A German operating theatre is pictured below. General anesthesia made careful, elaborate surgery feasible.

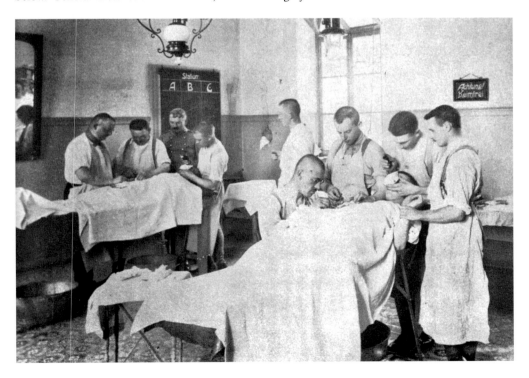

Captives. Russian prisoners marching toward a prison camp [above]. German prisoners on their way to a Russian prison camp [below].

The first Russian Revolution. The **Tsar** [left] was deposed early in 1917. Note the guards in the background. He was replaced by a provisional government in which a leading figure was **Alexander Kerensky** (1881-1970) [saluting on the right]. He is extorting the troops to continue the war.

Revolutions. The second Russian revolution [above] began with an armed uprising in Petrograd in which the Lenin's Bolseviks seized contol of the government. The Germans had brought Lenin back from exile in Switzerland. The German revolution began with uprisings against the Kaiser's government [below]. When he abdicated, power was assumed by the Social Democrats, the largest party in the Reichstag. Then there was some street fighting against Bolseviks and right-wing zealots. Friedrich Ebert (1871-1925), a former trade union leader, became the first president of the German Republic.

American Peacemakers. **Woodrow Wilson** (1856-1924) [left] was a professor, university president, and then governor before he was elected president in 1912. Forced to fight by the U-boat campaign, he proclaimed a 'war to end war'. He proposed Fourteen Points as a basis for a just peace and a League of Nations to prevent future conflicts. The Central Powers all requested armistices on the basis of his Points. At the Peace Conference Wilson sacrificed many of his Points to obtain the League, which was narrowly rejected by the United States Senate. **Edward M. House** (1858-1938) [right] was Wilson's confidant. A wealthy businessmen and political aficionado, he never ran for office. He wrote much of the Covenant of the League of Nations and took Wilson's seat at the Peace Conference when the president was back visiting the United States. Their friendship ended when House wanted to compromise with the Senate over the League and Wilson's health was giving way, which profoundly altered his behaviour.

The Big Four. The leading figures at the Peace Conference were **Lloyd George** [left], **Vittorio Orlando** (1860-1952) [second from left] , the Italian prime minister, **Clemenceau** [second from right], and **Wilson** [right]. Orlando was in a weak position, because Italy was bankrupt and depended on the others. He walked out for a time, but failed to obtain most of the territory the Italians had been promised. The Big Four did their hard bargaining in camera. Germans were were permitted to appear at the Conference only when invited to answer specific questions and had to respond to the draft of the treaty by written statements. The first of the Fourteen Points was: 'Open covenants of peace, openly arrived at, after which there shall be no private international understandings of any kind but diplomacy shall proceed always frankly and in the public view.'

The fate of the German High Seas Fleet. Above, the Fleet enters the British Naval Base at Scapa Flow. One of the provisions of the armistice was: 'German surface warships which shall be designated by the Allies and the United States shall be immediately disarmed and thereafter interned in neutral ports or in default of them in allied ports to be designated by the Allies and the United States.' Seventy warships were ordered to Scapa Flow. On 21 June 1919 the Germans scuttled all of the interned warships. Pictured right is the superstructure of the sunken battleship *Hindenburg* extending above the surface at Scapa Flow. It did not bode well for the future.

Staff officers played crucial roles in the War; here are two that subsequently rose to the heights. Général de Division **Maxime Weygand** (1867-1965) [left] was Foch's right hand man. When the German blitzkrieg struck France in 1940 he was called from Syria to take command of the French Army— too late to turn the tide. He sought an armistice and became the Vichy government's commander in North Africa. After the Allied landings in Africa he was a German prisoner for the remainder of the war. Colonel **George Catlett Marshall** (1880-1959) [right] was responsible for writing the stack of orders that shifted the US Army from facing east, toward San Michel, to facing north, toward the Argonne Forest. In World War II he was chief of the US staff and then became secretary of state (1947-49), initiating the program that bears his name for restoring the economies of both victors and vanquished in Europe (the USSR refused to participate). A model of how to make peace.

1917 ON THE WESTERN FRONT

The French still held most of the length of the front[9]. The Allies outnumbered their opponents [9,10].

The Western Front 4/1/1917
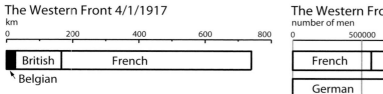

The Western Front 4/1/1917
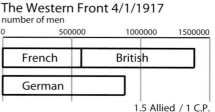

General Robert Nivelle had successfully nibbled back some of the German ground gains at Verdun, and spoke fluent English. He asserted that he could win the war by breaking through with the new French tanks and by skilled use of artillery, including their new 155mm guns (page 19). He concentrated fire on narrow lanes through which the infantry advanced behind a rolling barrage. Joffre was kicked upstairs and Nivelle was given command of the French Army.

The start of his plan was a limited British attack at Arras, to draw German reserves north (map on page 66)[73]. Then the French northern army would break through in the valley of the Somme: their line of attack is shown on the map by arrows. Simultaneously, the French central army would break through along the River Aisne, between Soissons and Reims, again shown by arrows. These simultaneous attacks would pinch off the Germans in the bulge protruding between the two spearheads; the German army would collapse and be driven from France.

Nivelle's ambitious scheme was undone when the Germans, for reasons of their own, pulled out of the bulge to a shorter defensive front—the newly constructed Hindenburg Line (the Allied name). Most of the hatched area on the map shows the German withdrawal. The line was the work of German engineers, French labourers, and Russian prisoners. They no longer dug deep dugouts, some of which had been death-traps in the Somme; instead the dugouts were shallower with reinforced concrete roofs and two exits. The Germans devastated the land as they withdrew. Now the planned northern French attack was impossible, but Nivelle was confident that his attack along the Aisne would suffice.

The enterprise started splendidly. The British attack from Arras broke completely through the German line. Ludendorff was so appalled he would not attend his birthday dinner. To the amazement of the Germans the British halted according to plan, and gave the Germans time to seal the breach.

NIVELLE'S PLAN

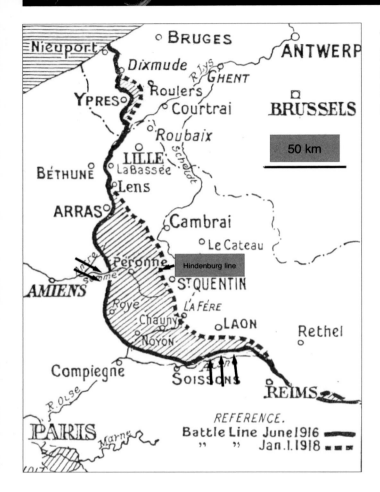

This map also shows the British gains at Ypres later in the year and Nivelle's advance along the Aisne[73].

To boost his troops' assurance, Nivelle circulated plans for the attack up to the front-line—where the Germans obtained their copy. The Germans had adopted elastic, in-depth defences[51]. They held their first trench line lightly. If taken, it was mercilessly bombarded by their own guns, which had the range precisely, and counter-attacked by infantry fighting through the maze of familiar trenches. For every three divisions at the front, two more were behind the line ready to counter-attack. (The German commander at Arras had not employed these tactics; he had concentrated his men in the first line. He was retired.) The Germans along the Aisne had four defensive positions; the final two were **8 to 19** km behind the front, beyond the range of enemy field artillery. Nivelle proposed to thrust through all four on the first day[26]. Each position consisted of **3 to 5** trench lines connected by a network of communication trenches, in which defenders and counter-attackers could manoeuvre.

NIVELLE'S ATTACK

The April weather was atrocious: bitter cold and sleet. Many of the French massed to attack had no shelter. Nivelle's African shock troops were especially demoralized by the freeze. The heavy casualties in the first hours overwhelmed the medical services. The French gains were far less than promised. Some units in the following waves refused to attack, and threatened their officers. A town was taken over and one unit proclaimed a new government. The French army seemed to be falling apart[50,67]. Ironically, French losses were no higher than in Joffre's Champagne offensive in the previous year[9]—but this time the attackers had been convinced that their commander knew what he was about.

Killed and missing April-17 - June-17

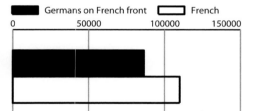

Killed and missing Sep-16 - Oct-16

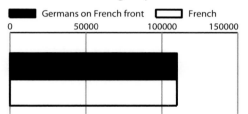

4 = number of fever thermometers in a hospital set up to receive 3,500 casualties from Nivelle's attack[50]

187 = number of German guns taken by Niville's offensive[50]

Most of the files about what occurred during the disorders are still French state secrets[68].

58 = number of French divisions in which there were disorders in 1917[50]

23,385 = number of French soldiers brought before military courts between May and October, 1917[50]

THE FRENCH RECOVERY

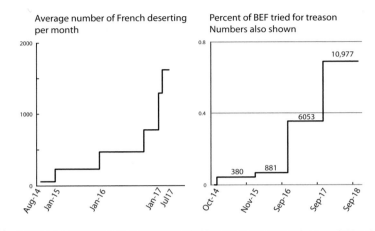

Average number of French deserting per month

Percent of BEF tried for treason
Numbers also shown

Some indication of the deterioration of French morale is given by the official figures for desertions[52,60].

However, British desertions also increased as the war went on, without major disorders[10].

180,000= number of soldiers' letters home read by French intelligence every week to assess morale[60]

Nivelle was replaced by Pétain. He stopped attacking, visited scores of regiments—he had a gift for talking with the men—improved food, leave, and living conditions, re-established discipline, and prosecuted hardcore mutineers. Astonishingly the Germans remained largely ignorant of the French disarray and were inactive in the West.

300%= increase in French soldiers' daily wine ration instituted by Pétain (to 750 ml)[60]

Casualties at Messines Ridge

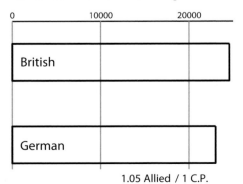

1.05 Allied / 1 C.P.

To deflect attention from the French turmoil, the British government allowed Haig to attack in Flanders. First he would seize the high ground east of Ypres—the Passchendaele ridge—then there would be amphibious landings along the coast to occupy the U-boat ports. In preparation for the main attack the British took the Messines ridge after blowing the German trenches sky-high by detonating **19** mines .

PASSCHENDAELE

423,000 kg = amount of high explosive in the mines exploded under the German lines on the Messines Ridge (1/32 of the power of the first atomic bomb dropped on Japan)[28]

The artillery bombardments destroyed the drainage system in the fields leading to Passchendaele and the rains poured down; the battle was fought knee-deep in mud. When the fighting died down in the autumn, the British had scarcely reached their objectives for the first day.

9.1 km = distance that the British advanced in 1917 to take Passchendaele

We have seen estimates of the casualties in a number of battles, but these figures may be misleading; the yearly summaries give a more reliable picture. When making their counts, historians define the extent of the battlefield and the dates for the battle, which can influence the results they report. Compare two estimates of the casualties at Passchendaele (I[27] and II[28]) with a joint British-German compilation of their casualties against one another during the months in question (III[10,48]). The data from the entire front suggests that Germans suffered less than what the historian's suggest. Throughout the battle Haig's intelligence staff assured him that German casualties exceeded British. In the Somme battle they determined that the enemy replaced a division when it sustained **30%** casualties[88]. They assumed that the rule still held, but in Flanders the Germans relieved their divisions when the staff judged the men unable to fight on effectively in the deplorable conditions, often with far fewer casualties[89]. Some writers still maintain the Germans lost more than the British[86].

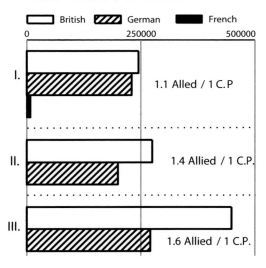

Passchendaele casualties

BRITISH AND GERMAN CASUALTIES

Wounded / killed on Western Front

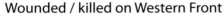
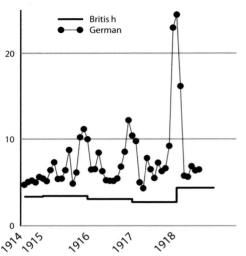

The British *Official History*[29] increased the number of wounded reported by the Germans by 30%, claiming that they did not log light wounds[30]. This hypothesis can be tested by comparing the ratio of wounded/killed on the Western Front, as recorded by the medical services of the two armies[17,18]. (The British figures were compiled by the year, the German by the month.) Contrary to the *Official History*, the Germans recorded a higher ratio of wounded to killed than the British. [The difference is statistically significant, Note I].

BRITISH TANKS AT CAMBRAI

The British did better with a surprise attack at Cambrai late in the year. After a brief hurricane bombardment, the infantry advanced behind tanks, which flattened the barbed wire and bridged the wide German trenches by dumping huge bundles of brushwood into them. They broke through the German trench lines, the bells rang in London, but they were not prepared to exploit their achievement. German reserves counter-attacked, driving the British back beyond their starting lines. Casualties on the two sides are said to have been approximately equal[27], but during the battle there were **1.5** British dead for each German killed on the Western Front[10].

324 = number of British tanks attacking at Cambrai, manned by **690** officers and **3,500** other ranks[61]

8.4 km = maximum advance of the British front at Cambrai[61]

PЙTAIN'S ATTACKS

Toward the end of 1917 Pétain delivered two set-piece, limited-objective, artillery-heavy attacks, largely to restore his men's confidence. The first recovered much of the ground lost to the Germans at Verdun; the second recaptured a French fort, Malmaison, along the Aisne. Total French casualties in the second attack were **12,500**[60].

Metres between guns in two of Pétain's attacks

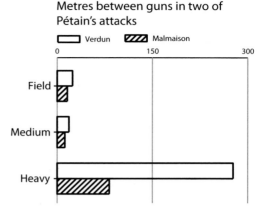

The Americans were building a new railway line running from the French Atlantic ports south of Paris, to the front south of Verdun, where their army would concentrate.

THE RUSSIANS COLLAPSE

The Tsar, who ruled as an autocrat, was forced to abdicate early in 1917. This enabled the Americans when they entered the war to claim that it was: 'A war to preserve democracy'. The provisional Russian government relied on the Allies for financing and promised to continue the war. They launched an abortive, costly offensive in the summer. In November Len-

Casualties at Riga

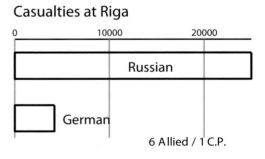

6 Allied / 1 C.P.

in's Bolsheviks seized power with the slogan: 'Bread and Peace'. They opened peace negotiations, but then stalled, waiting for the revolution to sweep over Western Europe. To prod them, the Germans seized the fortress city of Riga in a lightning attack across a river **350 m** broad[14]. Then they launched an amphibious assault on the island of Oesel, at the mouth of the waterway leading to Petrograd. They landed **23,000** men and **5,000** horses[42]. Most of the defenders melted away.

Throughout the war the Germans deployed fewer men in the East than in the West. With the Russian collapse they began to transfer the youngest, fittest men to the Western Front[18].

THE GERMANS MOVE WEST

Millions of German troops on two fronts

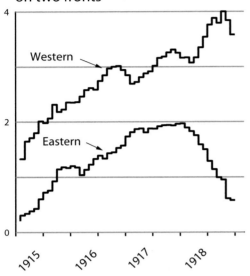

German casualties in the East were consistently lower than in the West, even taking into account the smaller troop levels in the East[18].

Thousands of German casualties on two fronts

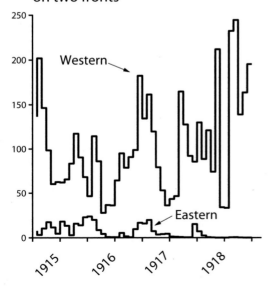

CASUALTIES IN THE EAST IN 1917

The Central Powers' casualties in the East in 1917 were much lighter than those of their disintegrating opponents[9,18].

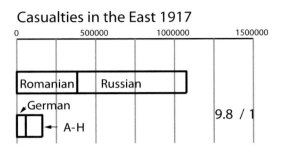

Casualties in the East 1917

ITALY IN 1917

The Italians continued to attack along the Isonzo throughout the summer, making some advances and taking the city of Gorizia but not breaking the line[20] (map page 41). In the eleven battles along the Isonzo the Italians invariably had the worst of it[20]. These battles each lasted about one month, so by the final attack the Italian casualty rate approached that of the British losses on the Somme[9,20]. Austro-Hungarian casualties on the Italian front were lower, but were a high percentage of their fighting men.

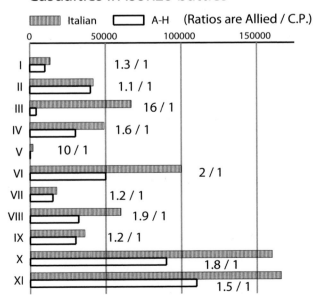

Casualties in Isonzo battles

CAPORETTO

Casualties and prisoners at Caporetto

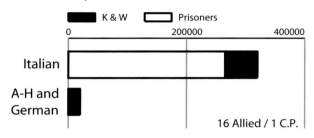

To keep the battered Austro-Hungarians in the war, late in the year Hindenburg sent German troops to Italy. A joint army, commanded by Otto von Below, a German, attacked on the northern part of the front, near Caporetto (map page 41), covering the enemy trenches in a dense gas cloud. They broke through and drove the Italians back to the river Piave where a front formed and was held with the help of French and British reinforcements[20]. (For distances see page 49).

110 km = Austro-German advance into Italy after the break though at Caporetto[20]

Casualties in Italy 1917

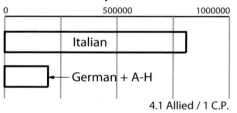

1917 was a disastrous year for the Italians[9], ending with a great swath of their country occupied. Nonetheless, public support for the war was bolstered: from then on there were few strikes or food riots and students rushed to enlist as storm troopers[20].

THE MIDDLE EAST IN 1917

After a disastrous early attempt in which their army was captured, the British advanced successfully up the Tigris and entered Baghdad in March 1917.

Falkenhayn was sent to command the Ottoman army, which was reinforced by a small German contingent. At first he planned to retake Baghdad, but gave it up when he was convinced that he would not be able to supply his army because the railway ran only to Aleppo (map on next page)[73]. Instead he concentrated in Palestine, where the British, led by Edmund Allenby, advanced northward by a series of clever manoeuvres, entering Jerusalem in December[9].

BAGHDAD AND JERUSALEM

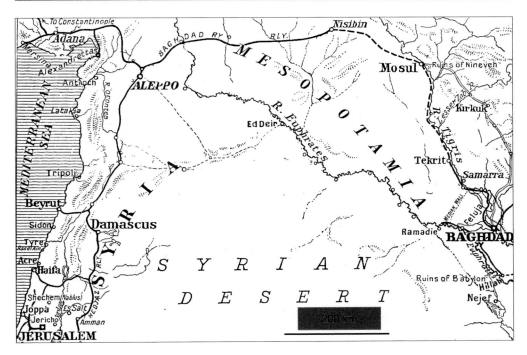

4/1 =

ratio of British attacking to
Ottomans defending Baghdad[67]

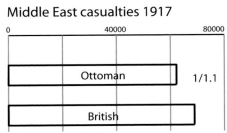

Middle East casualties 1917

	0	40000	80000
Ottoman			1/1.1
British			

PEACE MOVES

During 1917 there were abortive efforts to end the war. Lord Lansdowne, a former British foreign secretary, argued for a peace conference; Prime Minister Lloyd George was not interested. The Reichstag passed a resolution calling for peace without annexations. It was pocket-vetoed by a new German Chancellor, nonetheless the deputies continued to vote the funds needed to fight the war. Clemenceau, an unwavering hawk, came to power in France, pledging 'To wage war, nothing but war'. When the Bolsheviks came to power in Russia they proposed a general peace conference. No one would agree to attend.

PEACE TREATIES IN EARLY 1918

Early in the year, the Russians and Romanians signed peace treaties with the Central Powers. The map shows the front at the end of the war in the east and the territorial provisions of the Treaty of Brest-Litovsk[73].

The peace treaty ceded Russian Poland and Lithuania to the Central Powers and left the former Russian provinces in the west to decide their own futures as wards of the Central Powers. The Bolsheviks preached self-determination, but were outraged when the opportunity was given. The Allies denounced these grabs, but after they won the war they did not return territory to the Russians.

Early in the year, President Wilson presented his ideas for a just settlement as a series of 'points'. Many ordinary people on both sides thought them eminently reasonable, but they were not endorsed by any other belligerent government. How, for example, could the blockading British endorse the 'freedom of the seas'.

THE WEST IN 1918

Now the Germans outnumbered the Allies on the Western Front. The French still held the longest length of Allied line[9], though part of their front was in the mountains, where there was relatively

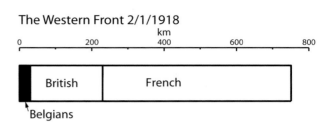

The Western Front 2/1/1918

little action. **250,000** American troops were in France[32], but they were busy training and building a rail and communications network from the Atlantic coast to Lorraine, where their army would be concentrated when it arrived.

The Germans determined to use their superior numbers to defeat the British Army, which they considered weaker than the French, by a series of massive attacks, each starting with a surprise hurricane bombardment, using many gas shells to suppress the enemy artillery. The first attack, 'Michael', was launched on 21 March with the most intense artillery bombardment of the war[14]. Preliminary bombardments for an attack had changed notably. Compare the British on the Somme[27] in 1916 with the Germans[14] for Michael in 1918. The German pioneers cut gaps in the enemy barbed wire for their infantry columns to slip through; the Allies smashed it with shells or crumpled it with tanks to make way for their waves of infantry.

Artillery preparation		
	British for Somme	**German for 'Michael'**
Hours of bombardment	168	5
Number of guns	1,537	6,608
Number of shells fired	1,500,000	3,200,000
Average shells/minute	8,929	640,000

Since about 58% of British casualties came from shell fire (page 22), we can estimate the number of shells fired to wound a Briton on one of the best documented days of the war[31].

1,070 =

number of aeroplanes the Germans used in the 'Michael' attack[31]

21 March 1918: the 'Michael' attack

British wounded = 10,000
Wounded by artillery = 5,800
Shells fired by Germans = 3,200,000
Shells fired to wound a man = 552

MICHAEL

The Germans attacked along the British front near the old Somme battlefields and smashed completely through[73]. The Allies were dumbfounded. The Germans broke through with adept tactics, not novel weapons. To meet the crisis the Allies gave supreme command to General Ferdinand Foch, who rushed up French reserves by motor lorry. They helped to stem the German advance, which formed a huge salient into the Allied line. The German advance was slowed when their troops paused to loot the riches of the British supply dumps. Michael was less successful than planned: the German set out to pinch-off a substantial fraction of the British Army but were checked by a stout defence along part of the line[78,79]. As they pushed as far as they might into Allied territory, they lengthened their own line and were unable to supply troops so far from their railheads across devastated countryside. German losses were higher than British[10].

Casualties facing one another: 21-Mar – 30-Apr

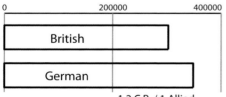

1.2 C.P. / 1 Allied

Undeterred, the Germans shifted artillery and reserves north. On 9 April they broke through the British and Portuguese lines in Flanders along the river Lys (map page 34), in one day recovering all the ground they had lost the year before, but failing to take the railway junction at Hazebrouck, their goal, which would have forced the Allies to evacuate Flanders[9] (Map page 28 on which the place names are in German spelling).

THE GERMAN ATTACKS IN 1918

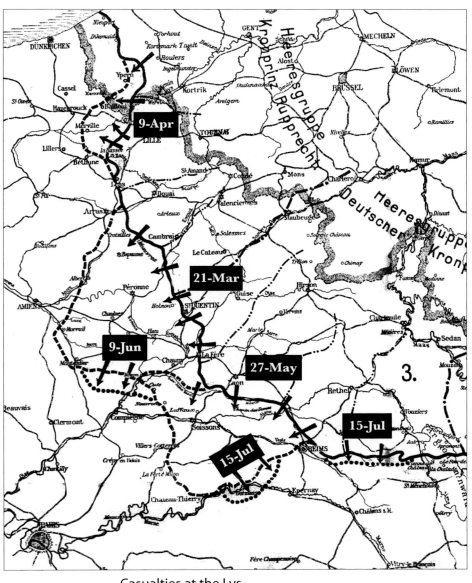

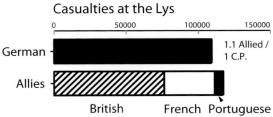

Casualties at the Lys

0	50000	100000	150000

German — (1.1 Allied / 1 C.P.)

Allies — British   French Portuguese

THE RESPONSE TO MICHAEL

The Americans were the Allied ace in the hole. The US was building its army by drafting men, while not allowing skilled workers to enlist, in an effort to amass one million troops. When the bad news arrived from France they accelerated their intake dramatically and set their goal higher[32].

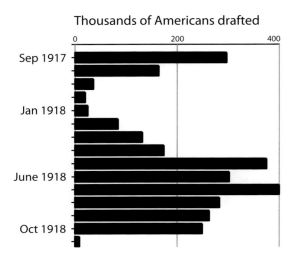

Thousands of Americans drafted

The Allies allocated scarce shipping to bring American troops to France[32]. The French and British asked for riflemen and machine gunners; they would supply the officers and NCOs. The US insisted on bringing over complete units, determined to have their own army. By now the BEF was short of infantrymen[10].

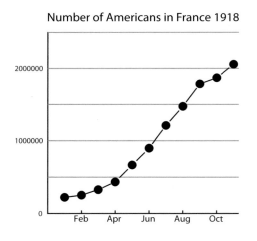

Number of Americans in France 1918

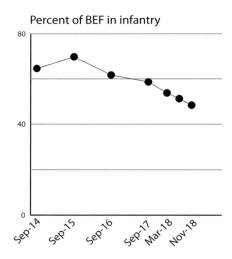

Percent of BEF in infantry

AMERICAN ARMS

The Americans produced their own rifles and machine guns[32]. Most of the latter were of a new, easily manufactured design, the Browning; they were not sent into battle until July for fear that they would be captured and copied. Aeroplanes, tanks and artillery took longer to get into production; French and British factories supplied most of the required heavy equipment.

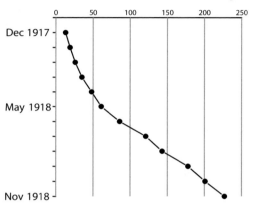

Thousands of American machine guns

THE THIRD GERMAN ASSAULT

The Germans still planned to deliver the knockout blow in Flanders, but first they would draw Allied reserves south. On 27 May they struck the Allied line along the Aisne (maps on pages 79 and 82)[9]. They broke through so readily and moved forward so rapidly that they altered their objective and drove toward Paris, pausing at the River Marne because they had difficulty getting supplies up to the new front-line.

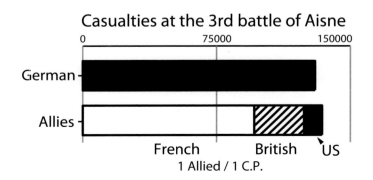

Casualties at the 3rd battle of Aisne

1 Allied / 1 C.P.

THE GERMANS REACH THE MARNE

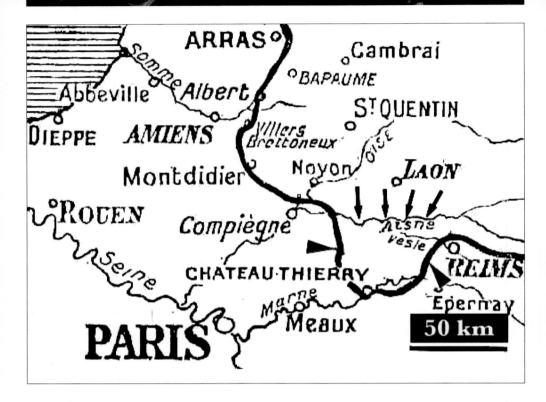

The black arrows show the direction of the German attack toward the Marne[73]. The triangles show the later French and American counter-attacks.

The next German attack was on 9 June, along the southern shoulder of the salient they had created with Michael[9], with the goal of broadening the Marne salient. The penetration achieved in this attack was much less than in its predecessors (page 83).

Casualties at Noyon-Montdider 9-14 June

	0	20000	40000
French			
German			

1.2 Allied / 1 C.P.

THE WEAKENING GERMAN ASSAULTS

By July the Americans and Italians had taken over part of the Allied front[9].

The Western Front 7/1/1918

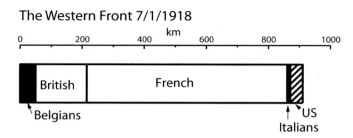

The distances the successive German attacks penetrated into the Allied lines reveal how they were becoming less effective as they lost men, hope, and energy, while the Allies were being reinforced and were learning how to cope with German assault tactics.

To take Paris the Germans needed additional railway lines to supply their troops on the Marne. On 15 July they attacked with two spearheads to pinch off the railway hub of Reims (map page 82). The French had learned where and when they were coming; the hurricane bombardment fell on almost deserted trenches and empty gun pits. When the German infantry reached the French line of

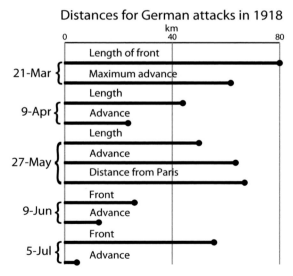

Distances for German attacks in 1918

resistance they were too far forward to have substantial artillery support. Their attack was completely stymied[9].

Now the Allies, urged on by Foch, began a counter-offensive. The French and Americans hit the flanks of the German salient projecting to the Marne (map page 82). The Germans were forced to abandon what they had won, and they lost many men as prisoners[9].

2nd BATTLE OF THE MARNE AND AMIENS

Casualties in the Second Battle of the Marne

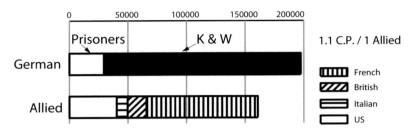

1.1 C.P. / 1 Allied

French

British

Italian

US

On 8 August the British surprised the Germans near Amiens[9]. Tanks advanced without preliminary bombardment while shells showered on the German artillery positions[10] which had been located by sound-ranging (page 55), even though they had been repositioned during a week too foggy for aerial reconnaissance. Entire units surrendered, leading Ludendorff to call it the 'black day' in the history of the German Army[74]. He was soon under psychiatric care and was replaced a few weeks later.

Casualties at Amiens

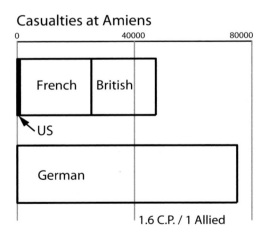

1.6 C.P. / 1 Allied

The Germans planned to retreat to a series of defensive lines, moving deliberately to give time to evacuate their wounded and stores. They hoped to prove to the Allies that it would be too costly to defeat the German army, so they could negotiate a tolerable peace. If necessary, the final defence line would be along the Rhine. It was a dream. Both their army and their nation were crumbling.

20 % = portion of the German troops being transported from East to West in 1918 who deserted along the way[66]

BRITISH SHELLS AND TANKS

The British artillery was now able to engage the enemy on equal terms, with enough guns and plentiful ammunition[10]. Winston Churchill had become minister of munitions.

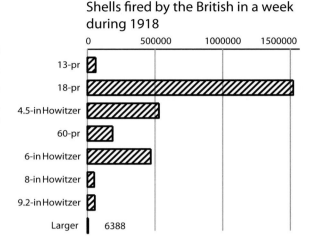

Shells fired by the British in a week during 1918

The Allies continued to attack and gain ground. The German front-line troops fought so manfully that the Allies were unaware that they were pushing forward against an ordered withdrawal. Haig feared that the war would go on into the next year because his tank force was so depleted[24].

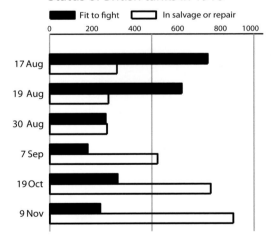

Status of British tanks in 1918

300 = number of Berlin armament factories struck on 16 April 1918[66]

2 = number of Ludendorff's 3 stepsons who died in the war as aviators

GAS USE IN 1918

**Shells fired at US 23rd Infantry
1-25 June 1918**

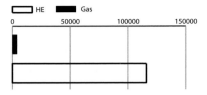

The records of a US regiment illustrate the effectiveness of gas as a weapon at this stage of the war[14].

Casualties from artillery fire

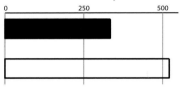

THE MEUSE-ARGONNE

**Casualties in the Meuse-Argonne
26 Sep – 11 Nov**

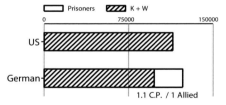

The major US attack was in the Meuse-Argonne sector, just west of Verdun[9]. They were pushing north to cut the main trunk railway between Germany and the Western front.

US casualties rose with each passing month; by August they were approaching the rate of British losses in the Somme[32] (page 47).

US monthly casualties in 1918

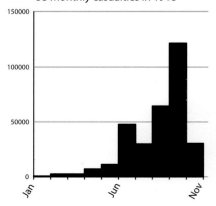

750,000 =

number of German troops estimated to be 'on strike' in November 1918[66]

FRENCH CASUALTIES

Accumulated casualties in France in 1918

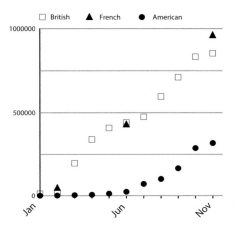

Nonetheless, French casualties still topped the Allied list[9,36,52,60].

THE END OF THE GERMAN EMPIRE

Scores of thousands of German troops were 'striking', milling about in the rear areas[66,78]. Civilians in the cities were starving, there was street fighting in Berlin, and the navy mutinied. Their allies were falling one by one. The Germans appealed for an armistice to negotiate a peace based on Wilson's Points. Wilson refused so long as the Kaiser ruled. The Kaiser and his son were forced to abdicate and a Social Democratic government took power—it was one of the most orderly revolutions in history, violently opposed only by Bolsheviks and staunch right-wingers. Hindenburg promised that the army would support the new government.

Armistices in 1918:

Bulgarian — 29 September
Ottoman — 30 October
Austro-Hungarian — 3 November
German — 11 November

The armistice (page 112) stipulated that all German troops must be over the German border within 14 days—stragglers would be made prisoner. The German staffs wrote the orders for each unit's march on each day; the stragglers returned to their units, supplies were directed to their stops, and **one million** men in the Imperial German Army withdrew in time and in good order.

87

THE END IN THE WEST

The Western Front 11/11/1918

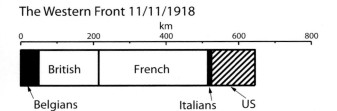

When the armistice came into force, the US held a significant part of the shortened front, but the French still held the longest stretch[9].

Casualties in 1918 on Western Front

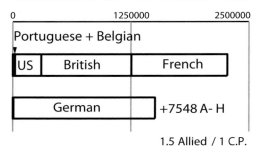

1.5 Allied / 1 C.P.

The Central Powers casualties in the West for 1918 included many prisoners[9].

THE ITALIANS VICTORIOUS

The Italian Army was reorganized under Armando Diaz. The Austro-Hungarians attacked unsuccessfully early in the year. By the end of summer the Czechs, Slovaks, Hungarians, Serbs, Croats, and Slovenes had left the Empire. The Austrians requested an armistice but it was payback time; the Italians and their Allies attacked in an operation they named Vittorio Veneto, capturing hundreds of thousands of prisoners before granting an armistice[9].

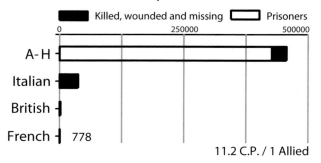

Casualties and prisoners at Vittoria Veneto

11.2 C.P. / 1 Allied

CASUALTIES IN ITALY IN 1918

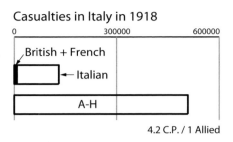

Casualties in Italy in 1918

4.2 C.P. / 1 Allied

THE BALKANS IN 1918

The Allies had landed troops at Salonica in Greece in 1916, where they sat in a fortified camp. They were reinforced by the remains of the Serbian army. Now they went on the offensive and pushed up through the rugged mountains toward Serbia and Bulgaria (map page 38). In September the Allied

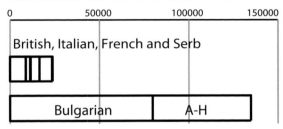

Casualties in the Balkans 1918

army, commanded by a French General Maurice Sarrial broke through the defensive fortifications and the Bulgarians left the war[9]. Cutting the rail line from Germany to Constantinople sealed the Ottoman fate.

THE END OF THE OTTOMAN EMPIRE

The British Army in Palestine coped brilliantly with long supply lines; they even piped water up from Egypt (map page 75). The Ottoman army was now almost entirely Turkish: the Arabs, Kurds and others had defected. The British, with Arab allies, encircled a large part of the remaining enemy forces. They

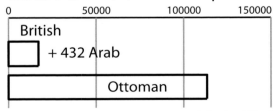

Casualties in Palestine & Iraq 1918

6.6 C.P. / 1 Allied

drove up into present-day Syria and took Damascus before the Ottomans surrendered[9,12].

89

FINLAND

Casualties in the Finnish civil war 1918

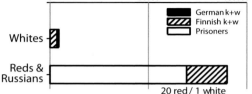

During 1918 nationalists in the emerging Baltic States, with some aid from the British or Germans, fought and defeated their Bolsheviks. In Finland there was a brief civil war between the nationalists and their German allies against the Bolsheviks and Russian troops stationed in the country[9]. The victorious nationalists were led by Gustav Mannerheim, who had been a successful Russian general. He later became regent and later president of Finland[79].

ALLIED MERCHANTMEN SUNK

Merchantmen sunk (1000's of tons)

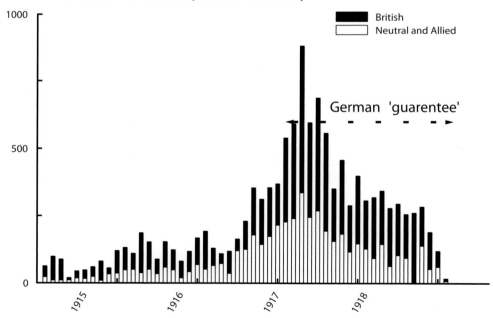

THE U-BOATS

When the Germans adopted unrestricted submarine warfare in February 1917 their navy promised to sink more than **600,000 tons** each month and to prevent US troops from crossing the Atlantic. Their failure is shown in the graph above. After initial German successes the Allies convoyed their merchant vessels, kept their people supplied with food and transported a large US army to France almost without loss[33,34]. This was as crucial for Allied victory as their successes on land.

400,000 = tons of shipping sunk by the most successful U-boat captain, Lothar de la Perier[35]

98 = number of U-boats based in Germany and Flanders in May 1918[35]

Submarine designers increased the fuel and the number of torpedoes carried[35]. Surface or submerged speeds did not rise substantially because they had not been able to develop powerful engines of reasonable weight.

Ship	Year	Length (m)	Speed surface (knots)	Submerged Speed (knots)	Torpedoes carried	Crew
U-17	1913	62.4	14.9	9.5	6	29
U-139	1916	92	15.3	7.6	19	86
U-142	1917	97.5	17.5	8.5	24	86

The Germans kept enlarging their U-boat fleet throughout the war[9], but never had anything like the number they could have used. They lost **178** U-boats, **515** officers and **4,894** other ranks[35].

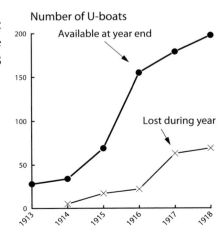

Number of U-boats

Available at year end

Lost during year

THE WORLD SHIPPING SUPPLY

Merchantmen in 1918 as percent of 1914

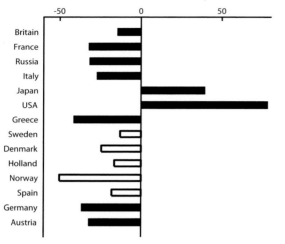

The U-boats reduced the shipping tonnage sailing under the British flag. However, by 1918 the total world supply of shipping had increased [9, 34].

CIVILIAN SUFFERING

Civilian life in Europe continued its downward spiral in 1918. There were more air raids on German cities. There were fewer on Allied cities, but Paris was bombarded by long range naval guns (page 20). The RAF was preparing a bombing force to assault German cities in 1919[48]. Food was short everywhere, but especially in the blockaded Central Powers. Urban Germans ate a small fraction of their pre-war fats and proteins[70]. Conditions were even more stringent in the Austrian cities.

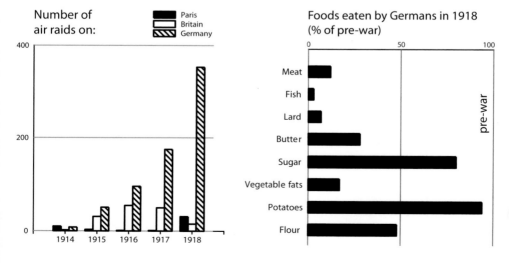

PRICES AND BIRTHS

Prices rose worldwide. In the warring countries wages fell far behind. Industrial workers were best off, but still were losing buying power. State employees and the retired were impoverished[69]. Many of the economic gains of the previous decades were swept away.

French prices and wages (1914=100)

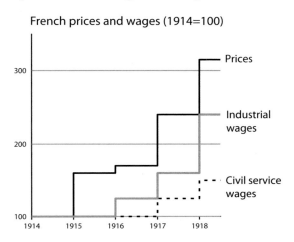

Birth rates fell, especially in Austria[2]. The British rate was the least affected.

Thousands of births per year

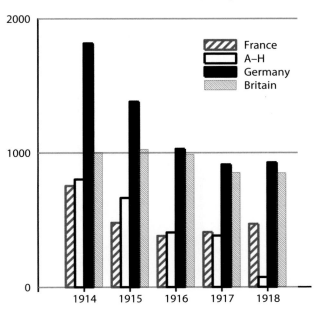

STUDENTS, STRIKES, AND PROFITS

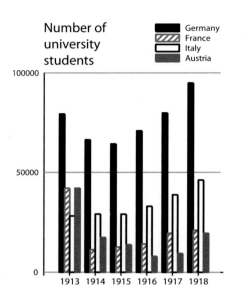

Number of university students

Germany
France
Italy
Austria

The number of students in the universities fell notably, especially in Austria. They were best sustained in Germany, and all began to rise in 1918 when veterans returned. Hindenburg had wanted the German universities shut, fearing that too many women were taking advantage of the war to become educated.

Strikes are one measure of worker grievances. The hours lost to strikes[9] never rose to the level of pre-war 1914. During the war strikes were broken by threats of military service, and many of the French workers were still in the army but assigned to industry, with the possibility of instant recall to the front. The profits of most arms firms increased, more than 10-fold in one of the examples shown[68].

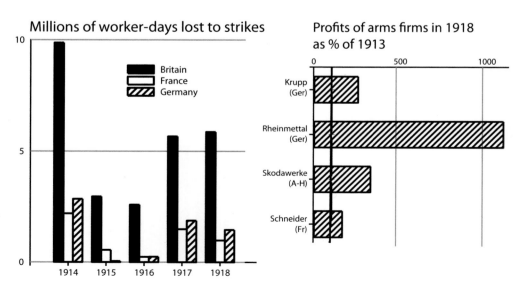

Millions of worker-days lost to strikes

Britain
France
Germany

Profits of arms firms in 1918 as % of 1913

SICK AND WOUNDED

The Great War was the first in which more men died in battle than from disease; the US figures are typical[36]. There was also substantial improvement in the survival of the wounded[36].

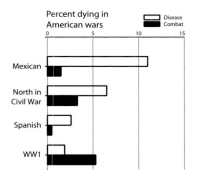

Throughout the war in every army more men were evacuated from the fronts due to illness than for wounds[17,18]. The large increase in the summer of 1918 was due to the worldwide pandemic of 'Spanish' influenza[18]. The virus struck the young, because they lacked immunity, and had a high death rate—something like **25 million** died worldwide[37], far more than were killed in the war.

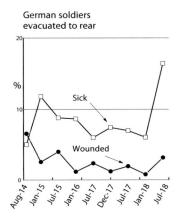

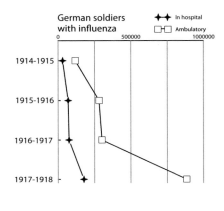

5,559 = number of American soldiers in US dying of influenza in the third week of October 1918

96 = seconds on average, between the deaths of French soldiers during the war

RETURNING TO DUTY

More of those hospitalized for illness returned to duty than those wounded[17]. All of the armies strove to reduce the number of men put out of action because of venereal disease. The best defence was to keep the troops in wild, mountainous country, like Macedonia[17].

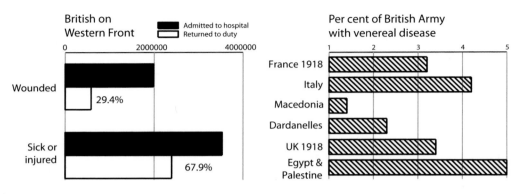

72 = seconds on average between German military deaths throughout the war

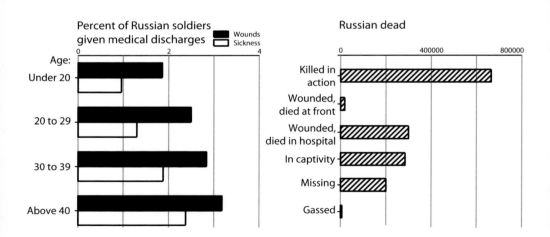

The Russian figures, not surprisingly, show that older men were more likely to be discharged after hospitalization than the younger[55]. **20%** of their fatalities were in prison camps[55].

OFFICER AND AVIATOR CASUALTIES

All of the armies struggled to cope with the need to replace officers. A higher percentage of officers were killed[10,17,18], a continual stream of replacements was required. The number of dead aviators increased greatly as the air war developed[10], but it was about equally dangerous to be a flying or a junior infantry officer, because flyers were relieved after a set number of missions.

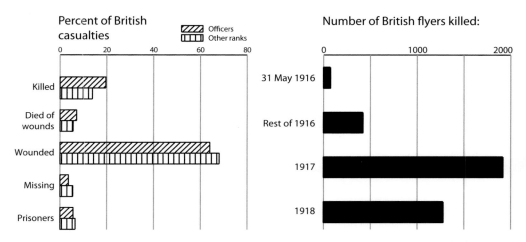

DANGERS ON DIFFERENT FRONTS

There were substantial differences in the casualties sustained on different fronts. The British data show this clearly[10].

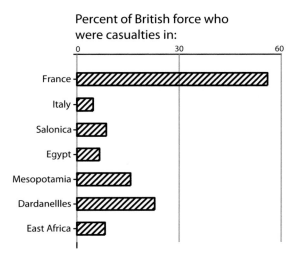

GERMAN JEWS IN THE WAR

In later years the Nazis claimed that the German Jews had shirked service, while those in the army had kept safe in the rear, thereby undermining the war effort. All lies. Jews made up **0.85%** of the German population. Since most were urban dwellers it is most instructive to compare their service with the similar number of Germans who were residents of Munich[72]. The percentages killed in action are identical. Overall the percentages of Jews serving in the army who were killed or decorated for bravery are indistinguishable from the German population as a whole, but a smaller percentage of Jews were officers[72].

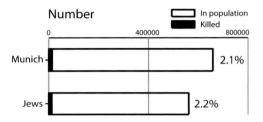

The German counts of the number of men hospitalized for nervous disorders are interesting for two reasons. First, that there was little change in the rate of hospitalization during the war. Second, that the rate was substantially higher in the reserve army in Germany than among troops in the field[18].

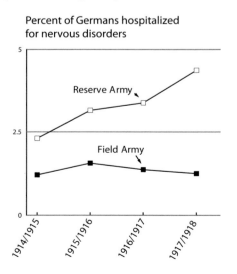

GAS AS A WEAPON

The poisonous gases used were heavier than air, so they sunk down into trenches; the scientists who introduced chlorine hoped to break the deadlock in the trenches and end the war. However, counter-measures are relatively easy. There were many casualties but relatively few died. The Russians suffered the most, because their defences were inadequate and their men poorly trained. Germany and France were the major users[38], but the British and Americans were planning to use huge quantities in 1919.

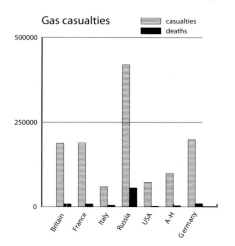

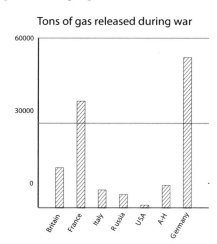

Gas shells were showered on gun positions, so artillerymen had the highest casualty rate[10, 14, 38].

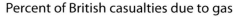

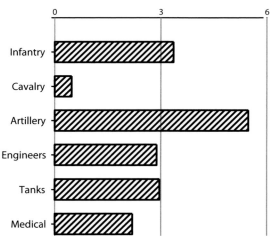

VEHICLES AND HORSES

British motor vehicles in France

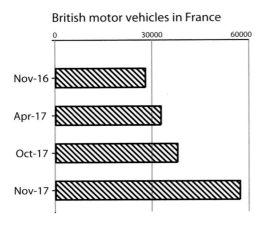

Initially the armies owned few motor vehicles. They mobilized private automobiles, often with the owner as chauffer, and requisitioned taxis and buses. Then they manufactured trucks and tractors, which took over more and more of the transport[10] (page 57). Nonetheless, horses and mules provided essential transport for all of the armies. Pre-selected horses were called up at the outbreak of the war. The level of wastage was high, so a continual stream of replacements was needed[39]. In the closing months many German and Austro-Hungarian divisions were so short of animals that they were immobile. In the British Army **9.5%** of the horses that were gas casualties died, compared to **44%** of the gunshot casualties[39]. The British lost **484,173** horses and mules in the war, **120,886** were battle casualties in France[39].

British horses in France

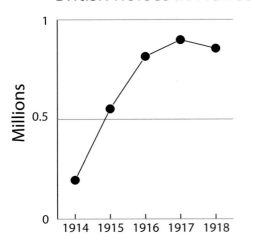

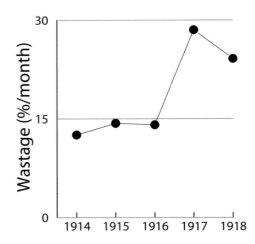

TOTAL CASUALTIES OF
THE MAJOR PARTICIPANTS

In the military a total of **6,360,000** men died of all causes and **8,375,000** were wounded[10]. This summary includes smaller countries not mentioned hitherto and is divided into two groups because the totals are so varied. In terms of percentage of the population killed the French suffered the most, followed by Austro-Hungary. The figure for Ottoman wounded is incomplete (*) and no figure is available for Romanian wounded. The Russians and Austro-Hungarians lost the largest numbers as prisoners.

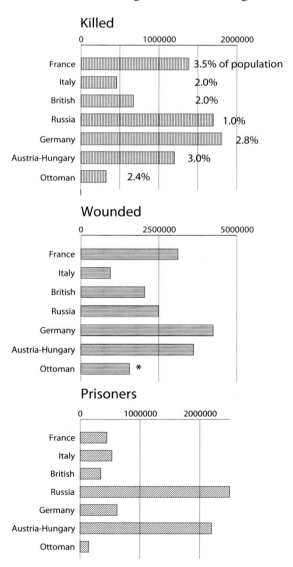

LESSER LOSERS

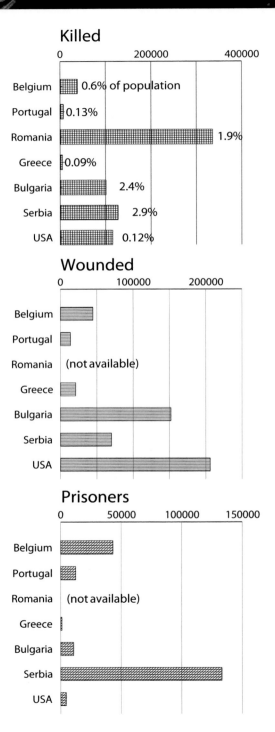

Killed

Belgium	0.6% of population
Portugal	0.13%
Romania	1.9%
Greece	0.09%
Bulgaria	2.4%
Serbia	2.9%
USA	0.12%

Wounded

Belgium	
Portugal	
Romania	(not available)
Greece	
Bulgaria	
Serbia	
USA	

Prisoners

Belgium	
Portugal	
Romania	(not available)
Greece	
Bulgaria	
Serbia	
USA	

CIVILIAN DEATHS

The figures for the number of civilians killed by the war were calculated by comparing death rates before and during the war[10,40]. The high number in Germany and Austria is attributed to the food blockade. When it was finally lifted, in April 1919, the body weight of town dwellers without special rations was down **15-20%**. A **30%** loss is lethal[40]. The British number includes civilian mariners. Roughly half of the Ottomans were Armenians who were slaughtered or died

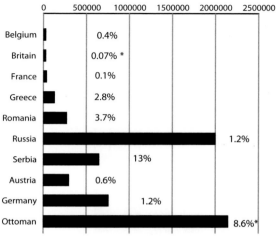

Number of dead civilians

when they were driven from their native soil because they were believed to favour the invading Russians.

FINANCING THE WAR

The war required governments to spend enormous amounts of money. US expenditures rose **25**-fold and German **15**-fold[10]. Like the British example, expenditures increased steadily and soon exceeded government income.

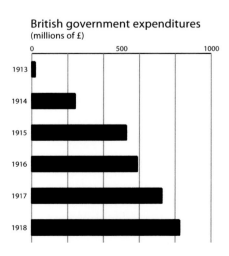

British government expenditures
(millions of £)

EXPENDITURES AND GOLD

Spending for civilian needs increased almost as much as direct military expenditures[41]. Money was spent abroad to buy what was needed, the British swung from a comfortable positive to a massive negative trade balance[2].

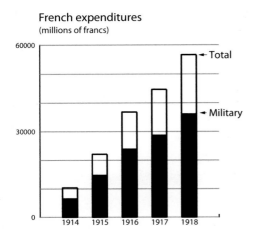

French expenditures
(millions of francs)

British balance of payments
(millions of £)

Changes in gold reserves
£ (millions)

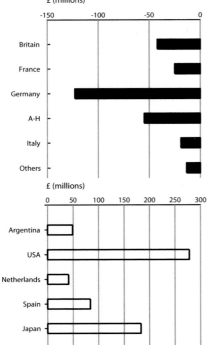

Some of the purchases had to be paid for in gold. The gold reserves of the buyers, which backed up their paper currencies, decreased while those of the sellers swelled[42].

FOOD

Industrial Europe imported food before the war. Production dropped when farmers were called to the colours, so imports had to be increased. The US and Argentina were major suppliers[43]. Food production in the US soared because the government guaranteed prices a year in advance and promised to buy everything produced.

Food prices: Jan 18 / Jul 14

US food exports
(millions of tons)

- Breadstuffs
- Meat & Fats

A major achievement was feeding the civilians in occupied Belgium and France. Industrial Belgium depended on imported food, which was cut off by the food blockade. Food was provided by a private organization, directed by Herbert Hoover, later a US president[79]. Much of it was paid for by the Allied governments and, as promised, the Germans let it go to the intended recipients.

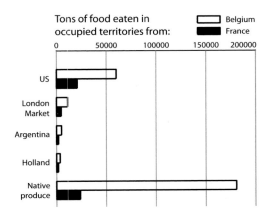

Tons of food eaten in
occupied territories from:

- Belgium
- France

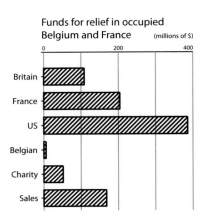

Funds for relief in occupied
Belgium and France   (millions of $)

£3,871,000 = cost of ammunition fired by the BEF in 24 hours starting at noon on 28 September 1918[10]

WAR LOANS

US War loans to:
(millions of $)

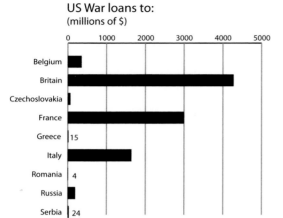

The imports of food and weapons by the Allies were sustained in part by massive loans from the US[2] and the British, who loaned **£2,087,000.**

MILITARY PAY

Military pay was a major expenditure [44,45,46]. Americans were best off, a captain made almost as much as a French colonel. In the German and French conscript armies privates were paid almost nothing. Not shown is a British grade below private, namely 'boy'. They were not allowed to serve overseas. It wasn't until the crisis of 1918 that 18-year-old Britons were sent to France to fight.

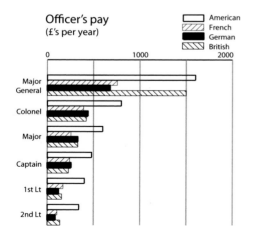

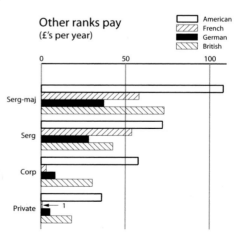

THE VALUE OF AN EYE

In the British Army pay scales varied substantially depending on assignment: officers in the household cavalry were better paid than the rest of the cavalry, but still needed outside funds to pay their way in peacetime. Flying officers with flight pay were best off. A value measure is shown by the gratuities given to British officers for loss of a limb or an eye; a field-marshal's was **26** times more valuable than 2nd Lieutenant's[44].

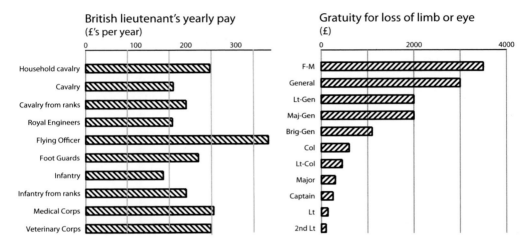

WOMEN WORKERS

The number of women employed in war industries skyrocketed, but often with agreements with the unions that they would only be allowed to do the work during the war.

THE FALL OF EMPIRES

Areas of losers before and after the war
(square miles)

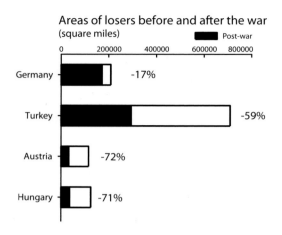

The war began because Serbia and Austro-Hungary were squabbling over lands that once were Ottoman; the Ottoman Empire had been shrinking for several centuries. The war finished both the Ottoman and Austro-Hungarian Empires. The Russian Empire lost Finland, the Baltic States, Poland, and, for a period, the Ukraine. They contained only **3.5%** of the empire's vast area, but they were well populated and well developed. Germany lost all of its overseas colonies, and in Europe ceded territory to Poland, Denmark, and France. The west bank of the Rhine and the coal-rich Saarland were occupied for years. Bulgaria lost **23%** of its land[56,57,58].

EXPANDING EMPIRES

The US opposed turning over the bits and pieces of the bygone empires to the victors as new colonies. Smuts came up with an agreeable sidestep: they were declared to be mandates of the new League of Nations (which the US never joined) and transferred to new masters in this guise[47]. We still suffer from the Ottoman collapse: Palestine, Iraq, and the Balkans remain serious trouble spots.

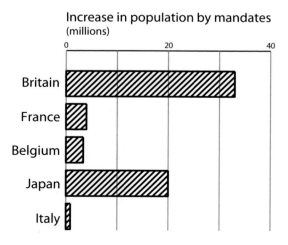

Increase in population by mandates
(millions)

THE EMERGENCE OF TURKEY

There were two peace treaties with the Turks. The Treaty of Sèvres in 1920 created an independent Armenia, an autonomous Kurdistan, and gave parts of Anatolia to the Greeks. The Allies occupied Constantinople and the Dardanelles. Kemal Atatürk and his comrades opposed the treaty, drove the Greek Army out of Anatolia, and stood face to face with the British troops along the straits[79]. The British gave way; the Treaty of Lausanne in 1923 finally ended the Great War, establishing the borders of modern Turkey.

The British backed out of Turkey because they no longer had the power to take what they wanted. The victorious European empires—British, French, and Belgian—were so weakened by the war that they began to crumble also.

The Japanese Empire did best for itself in the Great War. They obtained mandates in China and in German possessions in the Pacific, had increased their hoard of gold (page 104), and suffered few casualties (page 33). After this victory they continued fighting to expand further, only to lose their empire in World War II.

27 = number of victorious powers signing the Versailles Treaty

SUCCESS IN BATTLE

The war in the West was dominated by artillery, barbed wire and trenches. Great battles were fought trying to break into or through the enemy lines. Some attacks, indicated by a *, succeeded, others failed. Examining the density of the artillery and the length of front at-

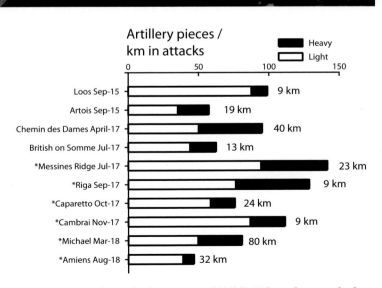

Artillery pieces / km in attacks

tacked does not reveal any consistent formula for success[10,14,48,54]. What the graph does not show is that all of these successful attacks were surprises. Generals were still needed, even in a war of material.

GERMAN EFFECTIUENESS

Killed and missing
on their front in France
(from 1915)

□—□ French
■—■ German

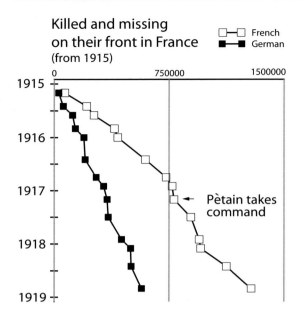

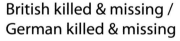

← Pètain takes command

The German Army was clearly the most effective. They completely out-matched the Russians. The French lost far more killed and missing than the Germans they faced. This was true in the first months of the war (page 27) and continued through-out. From 1915 to early 1917 about **2.2** Frenchmen were lost for every German opposing them[5,10,48]. After Pétain took command the rate of killing decreased and for this period **1.1** Frenchmen were lost per Ger-man. In 1918, the ratio rose again to about **2.8/1**.

THE IMPROVEMENT OF THE BRITISH ARMY

British killed & missing /
German killed & missing

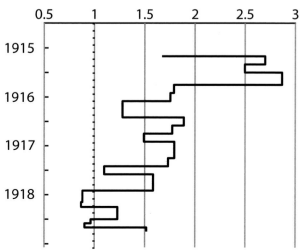

At first the British lost more than **2.5** men for each German facing them, but as the war went on odds improved, and during the German attacks of 1918 there were months in which German losses exceed-ed British[10,48]. [The decrease in the British/German ratio is statistically significant; Note II]. Nonetheless, as Travers has argued persuasively, the British did not win the war, the Germans lost it[25].

PERFORMANCE IN THE AIR

Another measure of effectiveness was the war in the air. The Allies lost **2.2** aircraft for every one lost by the Central Powers[10,21]. German military doctrine encouraged initiative, flexibility, and individual responsibility, and demanded close attention to every detail. Their training, from the highly educated general staff down to privates in the infantry, was excellent.

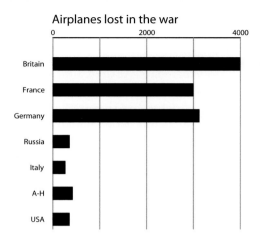

Airplanes lost in the war

HINDENBURG

Initially the German high commanders were unworthy of their army, but then Hindenburg, Ludendorff, and Mackensen provided leadership superior to their opponents. The Germans squandered their superiority in the field by the failure of their political leadership[49], which gave the military too much leeway in decisions beyond their competence. Their greatest blunders were unrestricted U-boat warfare, which brought in the US, and continuing their offensives in 1918 after the strategic failure of Michael. The Germans gambled for total victory and came close to total defeat.

2 = number of times Hindenburg was elected President of Germany. Ludendorff was decisively defeated when he ran

STARVATION AND THE ARMISTICE

The Armistice of 11 November 1918 eliminated any realistic prospect for Germany to resume the war. It also extended and made the food blockade more stringent, so urban Germans and Austrians continued to starve for months, leaving a further residue of hate and bitterness[38].

THE RESIDUE OF HATE

Some provisions of the Armistice With Germany

- Evacuation of Belgium, France, Alsace-Lorraine, Luxemburg within fourteen days. Any remaining German troops will become prisoners of war.

- Surrender of five thousand guns (2,500 heavy, and 2,500 field), 25,000 machine guns, 3,000 minenwerfer, 1,700 airplanes (including all night bombers and Fokker D7 fighters).

- All German troops to withdraw from Russia at a time decided by the Allies.

- Surrender to the Allies and United States of all submarines.

- The blockade is to remain unchanged.

Arguably, on the Allied side the French hated the most. They suffered enormous human losses and a great swath of their beloved country was smashed into tortured wasteland and rubble. They organized the peace conference and their fury is documented by the dates they selected for the milestones in the proceedings. Most Europeans had lost so much in the war and hated so intensely that it is improbable that any group of statesmen could have devised a peace that would last for long.

DATE IN 1918	ACTION	ANNIVERSARY OF
January 18	Opening of Versailles Peace Conference	Formation of Second German Reich in 1871
May 7	Draft treaty given to Germans for comment	Sinking of Lusitania
June 28	Signing of treaty	Archduke's murder

ECONOMIC STAGNATION

The graphs show the cold facts of the loss of life, health, and treasure due to the Great War. They cannot convey the profound transformation in the European ethos, which in four terrible years tumbled from hope and pride to sourness and despair—primed to be led into another tragedy. The growth of personal income that had enhanced life in Western Europe in the 19th century levelled off with the Great War, and started to rise again only in the late 1930s when spending on armaments primed the economies[6]. After the dictators finally fell in mid-century, Western Europe finally returned to the path started on in the 19th century.

The home countries of the remaining empires had grown rich over the years—their colonies had not; take India for example[6,87]. After the First and Second World Wars resources were poured into efforts to keep colonies in line. They failed. One by one, the colonies became independent[87].

GDP / capita (in 1990 $)

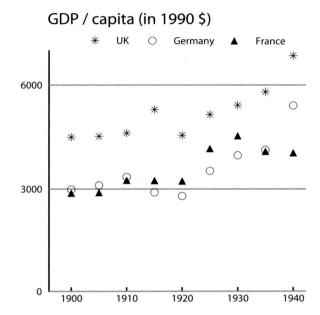

GDP / capita (in 1990 $)

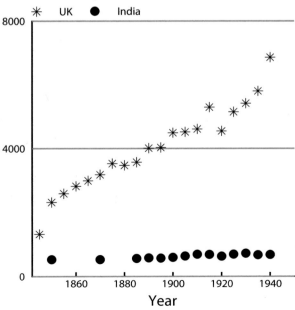

TERRITORIAL CHANGES IN EUROPE

This map, with labels in French, shows the changes in European borders following the war. Pre-war Germany is shaded, crosshatching shows areas ceded to the Danes, Poles, Belgians, and French (number 4 points to the Saar industrial region that was occupied by the French until 1935). The map does not show that the left bank of the Rhine was occupied by Allied troops who left in three stages ending in 1930. The breakup of Austria-Hungary expanded Romania and established Czechoslovakia, Yugoslavia, and Poland. Bulgaria lost territory to Greece.

THE DISABLED

British servicemen disabled by

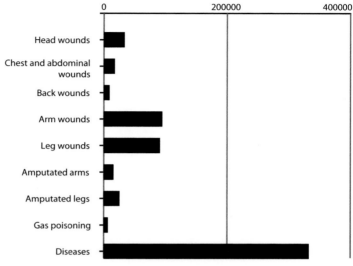

Millions of men were disabled by the war. The British tally of those receiving disability awards shows the reasons[17]. Note that only **1.1%** of the total were disabled by gas.

621,972 = British servicemen receiving disability

A breakdown showing the classes of medical conditions leading to disabilities.[17] The records are incomplete about the number suffering from shell shock; the Royal Army Medical Corps was reluctant to regard it as a syndrome.

British servicemen disabled by medical conditions

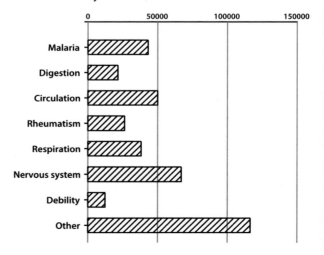

THE ADVANCE OF SCIENCE

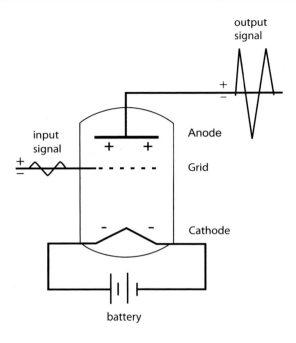

Arguably, amplifiers were the most important scientific advance made during the war. The simplest amplifying vacuum tube valve is diagrammed. There are three structures within an evacuated glass tube. Electrons are produced at the cathode, a wire heated by an electrical current provided by a battery. The anode is a metal plate that is given a positive electrical charge to attract electrons. The grid is a fine metal meshwork between the cathode and anode. The potential on the grid determines how many electrons flow from the cathode to the anode. In the illustration, a small alternating electrical potential applied to the grid leads to an amplified signal on the anode.

Amplifying vacuum tube valves were just being developed in 1914, primarily in the US. By 1917 the French were producing 1700 vacuum valves per day.[92]

Amplifiers dramatically improved radio communications, increasing the strength of the signal sent by transmitters and amplifying faint signals picked up by receivers. Amplifiers were essential for the echo-location of submerged U-boats—ASDICs or sonar—which the French and British had operational by the very end of the war.[93]

1,000,000 = number of vacuum tube valves produced in the US during the war [Tyne]

116

WOUND SHOCK AND TRANSFUSIONS

Some wounded men become ashen, listless, and unable to tolerate surgery. British medics discovered that the shocked have a low blood pressure, which is likely to continue to fall until death.[94]

By 1918 some shocked patients were saved by transfusions, either of human blood from a donor or with a solution of gum acacia, a plant product containing molecules the size of plasma proteins. It was like raising the dead.[95] Thousands of men were treated, but astonishingly, no records were kept of how many were transfused or the success rate.

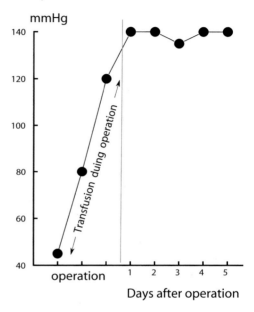

Systolic blood pressure in a patient with wound shock

THE RUSSIAN CIVIL WAR

The armistices in Western Europe did not end the fighting in the Russian Civil War or in the Polish-Soviet War.[96]

1,000,000 = estimate of number of Red Army troops killed in the wars [96]

500,000 = estimate of number of troops in the White armies killed in the civil war [96]

18,500,000 = estimate of number of civilians who died as a result of the Russian Civil War [96]

THE RUSSIAN CIVIL WAR

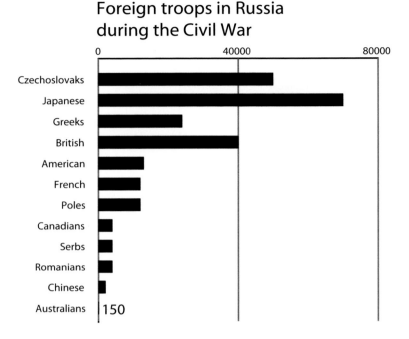

Foreign troops in Russia during the Civil War

Large numbers of troops from other nations were in Russia during the Civil War. Some were there to protect depots of stores that had been provided to the Russians during the war. Others had broader objectives. The British provided air support for White Armies. The Japanese aspired to occupy border regions. The Czechoslovaks were former prisoners of war who had been mobilized to fight on the Allied side; they fought their way out of Russia in a memorable campaign.

60,000 = estimate of Polish Army dead in the war with the Soviets, 1919-1921 [96]

GERMAN POST-WAR MILITARY PLANNING

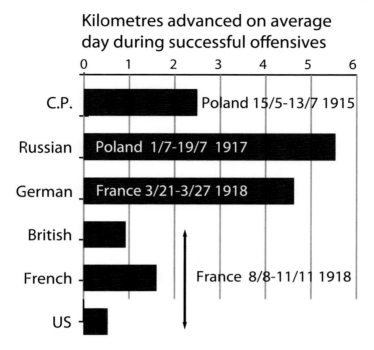

Kilometres advanced on average day during successful offensives

C.P.	Poland 15/5-13/7 1915
Russian	Poland 1/7-19/7 1917
German	France 3/21-3/27 1918
British	
French	France 8/8-11/11 1918
US	

In the 1920s the armies prepared for the next war. Reviewing the history of the war, the Germans saw that even the most successful advances in the later years of the war were well short of the **18.6 km/day** marched by the German Army during the sweep to the Marne[97]. Therefore they worked on regaining mobility[98]. Initially their field exercises were performed with trucks carrying signs indicating that they were tanks or personnel carriers that could move cross country—weapons prohibited by the Versailles Treaty. Over the years they obtained the equipment they needed to put their ideas to the test.

38.5 km/day = average distance travelled by German spearhead across France to Abbeville, 10-20 May 1940

0.074 km/day = average advance by the British Army at Passchendaele 15 June-7 December 1917

COMBATANTS KILLED IN THE TWO WORLD WARS

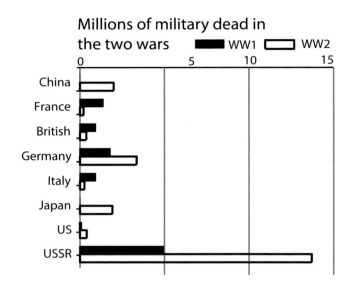

Millions of military dead in the two wars ■ WW1 ☐ WW2

The French, Italians, and British Commonwealth had fewer military dead in World War II than in World War I. All of the other major powers had greater losses, especially the Chinese and Japanese, because Asia was a major theatre of war[99].

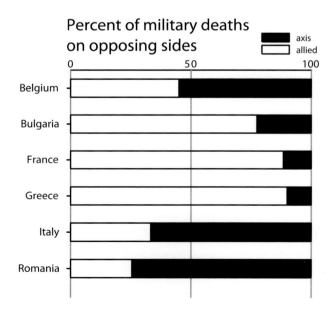

Percent of military deaths on opposing sides ■ axis ☐ allied

One of the unusual features of World War II was the number of countries that incurred military deaths fighting on both the Axis and the Allied sides. In World War I only Austria-Hungary had significant numbers of its citizens fighting on the opposing side.

CONCLUSION

To conclude we will return to the first graph, showing the population of the world, which began to grow exponentially after the Second Agricultural Revolution. Despite the carnage of the war and the ferocity of the influenza epidemic the number of inhabitants did not decrease: from 1910 to 1920 the human race added another 110 million people. Similarly population grew throughout World War II and continues unchecked to the present day.

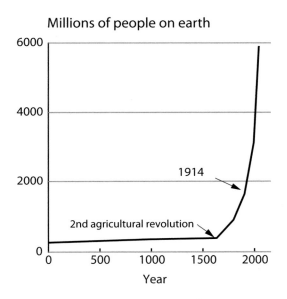

The wars continue and keep in mind:

> War's a brain-spattering, windpipe-slitting art,
> Unless her cause by right be sanctified.

Byron, *Don Juan, Ninth Canto IV.*

SOURCES

1. Fogel, R. W. (2004). *The Escape from Hunger and Premature Death, 1700-2100*. Cambridge, Cambridge University Press.

2. Mitchell, B. R. (1998). *International Historical Statistics: Europe 1750-1993*. London, Macmillan .

3. Erickson, C. (1976). *Emigration from Europe 1815-1914*. London, Adam & Charles Black.

4. Wadsworth, A. P. (1955). *Newspaper circulation 1800-1954*. Trans. Man. Stat. Soc. 1-12.

5. Hubert, M. (1931). *La Population de la France pendant la Guerre*. Paris, Les Presses Universitaires de France.

6. *www.ggdc.net/maddison/*

7. Wawro, G. (1996). *The Austro-Prussian War*. Cambridge, The University Press.

Howard, M. (1961). *The Franco-Prussian War*. London, Rupert Hart-Davis.

8. Hobson, J. M. (1993). 'The Military-Extraction Gap and the Wary Titan: The Fiscal Sociology of British Defence Policy 1870-1913.' *Journal of European Economic History*.

9. Gray, R. and C. Argyle (1990). *Chronicle of the First World War*. New York, Facts On File.

10. War Office (1922). *Statistics of the Military Effort of the British Empire in the Great War*. London, HMSO.

11. *War Facts and Figures*. (1914). London, British Dominions Insurance.

12. Erickson, E. J. (2001). *Ordered to Die: A History of the Ottoman Army in the First World War*. Westport, CT, Greenwood Press.

13. Golovine, G. N. N. (1931). *The Russian Army in the World War*. New Haven, Yale University Press.

14. Zabecki, D.T. (1994). *Steel Wind. Colonel Georg Bruchmüller and the Birth of Modern Artillery*. London, Praeger.

15. Hogg, I. V. (1998). *Allied Artillery of World War One*. Hungerford, Crowood.

16. Bull, G. V. and C. H. Murphy (1988). *Paris Kanonen – the Paris Guns (Wilhelmgeschütze) and Project HARP*. Hereford, Mittler.

17. Mitchell, M. T. J. and M. G. M. Smith (1997). *Medical Services. Casualties and Medical Statistics of the Great War*. London, Imperial War Museum.

18. Germany (1935). *Sanitätsbericht über das Deutsche Herr-Deutsches Feld-und Besatzungsherr-im Weltkriege 1914/1918*. Berlin.

19. Gibb, A.D. (1924). *With Winston Churchill at the Front*. London, Gowans and Gray.

20. Schindler, J. R. (2001). *Isonzo. The Forgotten Sacrifice of the Great War*. Westport, CT, Praeger.

21. Jones, H. A. (1937). *The War in the Air*. Oxford, Clarendon Press.

Kennett, L. (1991). *The First Air War*. New York, Macmillan.

SOURCES

22. Bragg, Sir L. W. (1971). *Artillery Survey in World War I*. London, Field Survey Association.

23. Wrisberg, E. von (1922). *Wehr und Waffen 1914-1918*. Leipzig, R. F. Koehler.

24. Stern, A. G. (1919). *Tanks 1914-18*. London, Hodder and Stoughton.
Fletcher, D. (2001). *The British Tanks 1915-19*. Ramsbury, Crowood Press.

25. Travers, T. (1992). *How the War was Won. Command and Technology in the British Army on the Western Front, 1917-1918*. London, Routledge.

26. Spears, E. L. (1939). *Prelude to Victory*. London, Jonathan Cape.

27. Johnson, J. H. (1995). *Stalemate: The Great Trench Warfare Battles of 1915-17*. London, Arms and Armour.

28. Prior, R. and T. Wilson (1996). *Passchendaele. The Untold story*. New Haven, Yale University Press.

29. Edmonds, J. E. (Editor), (1926-1947). *Official History: Military Operations, France and Belgium*. London, HMSO.

30. Williams, M. J. (1964). 'Thirty percent: a study in casualty statistics'. *Royal United Services Institute Journal* 109: 51-55.

31. Middlebrook, M. (1983). *The Kaiser's Battle. 21 March 1918: The First Day of the German Spring Offensive*. London, Penguin.

32. Ayres, L. P. (1919). *The War with Germany*. Washington, Government Printing Office.

33. Newbolt, H. (1931). *Naval Operations*. London, Longman, Green & Co.

34. Hurd, S. A. (1929). *The Merchant Navy*. London, John Murray.

35. Gray, E. A. (1972). *The U-boat War 1914-1918*. London, Leo Cooper.
Rössler, E. (1981). *The U-boat*. London, Arms and Armour Press.

36. Love, A. G. (Editor) (1925). *Medical Department of the United States Army in the World War. XV, Statistics*. Washington, Government Printing Office.

37. 'Influenza epidemic of 1918-19.' *Encyclopedia Britannica*. 2006. Encyclopedia Britannica Online.

38. Van der Kloot, W. (2004). 'April 1915: Five future Nobel prize-winners inaugurate weapons of mass destruction and the academic-industrial-military complex.' *Notes and Records of the Royal Society*. London 58: 149-160.

39. Blenkinsop, T. J. and J. W. Rainey (Editors) (1925). *Official History of the Veterinary Service*. London, HMSO.

40. Starling, E. H. (1920). 'The food supply of Germany during the war.' *Journal of the Royal Statistical Society* 83: 225-254.

41. Jèze, G. and H. Truchy (1927). *The War Finance of France*. New Haven, Yale University Press.

SOURCES

42. Gilbert, M. (1994). *Atlas of World War I*. New York, Oxford University Press.

43. Hoover, H. (1952). *Memoirs of Herbert Hoover 1874-1920*. London, Hollis and Carter.

44. War Office (1914 (reprinted 1917)). *Royal Warrant for the Pay, Appointment, Promotion, and Non-effective Pay of the Army*. London, HMSO.

45. War Office General Staff (1914). *Handbook of the German Army*. London, Imperial War Museum.

46. War Office General Staff (1914). *Handbook of the American Army*. London, Imperial War Museum.

47. Keynes, J. M. (1919). *The Economic Consequences of the Peace*. London, Macmillan.

48. Churchill, W. S. (1939). *The World Crisis 1911-1918*. London, Odhams Press.

49. De Gaulle, C. (2002). *The Enemy's House Divided*. Chapel Hill, University of North Carolina Press.

50. Watt, R. M. (1964). *Dare call it Treason*. London, Chatto & Windus.

51. Wynne, C. G. C. (1940). *If Germany Attacks. The Battle in Depth in the West*. London, Faber and Faber.

52. Doughty, R. A. (2005). *Pyrrhic Victory. French Strategy and Operations in the Great War*. Cambridge MA, Harvard University Press.

53. Stone, N. (1998). *The Eastern Front 1914-1917*. London, Penguin.

54. Haythornthwaite, P. J. (1990). *The World War One Source Book*. London, Arms and Armour.

55. Kohn, S. and A. F. Meyendorff (1931). *The Cost of the War to Russia*. New Haven CT, Yale University Press.

56. *The Statesman's Year-Book – 1914*. London, Macmillan.

57. *The Statesman's Year-Book – 1920*. London, Macmillan.

58. *The Statesman's Year-Book – 1925*. London, Macmillan.

59. Brown, I. M. (1998). *British Logistics on the Western Front 1914-1918*. Westport CT, Praeger.

60. Clayton, A. (2003). *Paths of Glory. The French Army 1914-18*. London, Cassell.

61. Liddell Hart, B. H. L. (1959). *The Tanks. Volume One 1914-1939*. New York, Frederick A. Praeger.

62. Chasseaud, P. (1999). *Artillery's Astrologers. A History of British Survey and Mapping on the Western Front 1914-1918*. Lewes, Mapbooks.

63. Samuels, M. (1995). *Command or Control?: Command, Training and Tactics in the British and German Armies, 1888-1918*. London, Frank Cass.

64. Gudmundsson, B. I.(1993). *On Artillery*. Westport CT, Praeger.

65. *www.nationalarchives.gov.uk/currency/*

66. Deist, W. (1996). 'The Military Collapse of the German Empire. The Reality behind the Stab-in-the-back Myth.' *War In History* 3: 186-207.

SOURCES

67. Tucker, S. C. (Editor) (1996). *The European Powers in the First World War. An Encyclopedia.* London, Garland Publishing.

68. Smith, L. V., S. P. Audoin-Rouzeau, and A. Becker (2003). *France and the Great War 1914-1918.* Cambridge, The University Press.

69. March, L. (1926). *Mouvement des Prix et des Salaires pendant la Guerre.* Paris, Les Presses Universitaires de France.

70. Hardach, G. (1977). *The First World War 1914-1918.* London, Alan Lane.

71. Strachan, H. (2001). *The First World War. Volume I. To Arms.* Oxford, Oxford University Press.

72. *http://www.germanjewishsoldiers.com/epilogue.php*

73. Modified from: The Times(1923). *The History of the War.* London, The Times.

74. Modified from: Ludendorff, E. (1919). *Ludendorff's Own Story.* New York, Harper and Brothers.

75. Modified from: Crown Prince William of Germany (1926). *My War Experiences.* London, Hurst and Blackett.

76. Hartcup, G. (1988). *The War of Invention. Scientific developments, 1914-18.* London, Brassey's Defence Publishers.

77. Chickering, R. (1998). *Imperial Germany and the Great War, 1914-1918.* Cambridge, Cambridge University Press.

78. Lutz, R. H. (1934). *The Causes of the German Collapse in 1918.* Stanford, Stanford University Press.

79. Van der Kloot, W. (2008). *The Lessons of War. The Experiences of Seven Future Leaders in the First World War.* Stroud, The History Press.

80. Great Britain (1920-22). *History of the Ministry of Munitions.* London, HMSO.

81. Farwell, B. (1987). *The Great War in Africa 1814-1910.* Harmondsworth, Viking.

82. Hordern, C. (Editor) (1941). *Military Operations in East Africa. August 1914-Sept. 1916.* London, HMSO.

83. Graff, H. J. (Editor) (1981). *Literacy and Social Development in the West, a Reader.* Cambridge, Cambridge University Press.

84. Palmer, A. (1965). *The Gardeners of Salonika.* London, Andre Deutsch.

85. Cassels, L. (1984). *The Archduke and the Assassin. Sarajevo, June 28, 1914.* New York, Stein and Day.

86. Corrigan, G. (2003). *Mud, Blood and Poppycock. Britain and the First World War.* London, Cassel.

87. Davis, L. E., and R. A. Tuttenback. (1986). *Mammon and the Pursuit of Empire. The Political Economy of British Imperialism, 1860-1912.* Cambridge, Cambridge University Press.

88. Sheldon, J. (2005). *The German Army in the Somme. 1914-1916.* Barnsley, Pen and Sword.

SOURCES

89. Sheldon, J. (2007). *The German Army at Passchendaele*. Barnsley, Pen and Sword.

90. Bridland, T. and A. Morgan (2003). *Tunnel-master and Arsonist of the Great War. The Norton-Griffiths Story*. Barnsley, Leo Cooper.

91. Charteris, J. (1931). *At G.H.Q.* London, Cassell.

92. Tyne, Gerald F. J. (1977). *Saga of the Vacuum Tube*. Indianapolis, Howard W. Sams.

93. Hackmann, William (1984). *Seek & Strike. Sonar, Anti-Submarine Warfare and the Royal Navy 1914-54*. London: Her Majesty's Stationery Office.
A brief, very high frequency sound pulse was emitted into the water from an array of oscillating quartz crystals. Any reflected sound changes the electrical potential across the crystal and was amplified to give an audible 'ping'.

94. Cowell, E. M. (1919) 'The Initiation of Wound Shock and Its Relation to Surgical Shock.' *Lancet* no. July: 1-27.

95. Bayliss, W. M. (1918) *Intravenous Injection in Wound Shock*. London, Longmans, Green & Co.

96. Mawdsley, Evan (1987). *The Russian Civil War*. London, Allen & Unwin.

97. The German and Russian advances are from maps in 74, the Allied advances are from maps in Boraston, J. H., ed. (1919) *Sir Douglas Haig's Despatches (December 1915 - April 1919)*. London & Toronto, J. M. Dent & Sons.

98. Citino, Robert M. (1999). *The Path to Blitzkrieg: Doctrine and Training in the German Army, 1920-1939*. London, Lynne Rienner.

99. *http://www.secondworldwar.co.uk/casualty.html;*
http://www.worldwar-2.net/casualties/world-war-2-casualties-index.htm.

NOTES

I. The probability that the difference is by chance very low, only 1.3 x 10-7.

II. The regression line has a slope of -0.031, with 95% confidence limits of -0.0173 and -0.0437, so it is highly probable that the British/German ratio was falling.